Life Lessons
WOMEN
in the
BIBLE

Rhonda Harrington Kelley

LifeWay Press
Nashville, Tennessee

ISBN 0-7673-3574-0

Dewey Decimal Classification: 220.92
Subject Heading: WOMEN IN THE BIBLE

This book is the text for course CG-0440 in the subject area
Personal Life in the Christian Growth Study Plan.

Order additional copies of this book by writing to Customer Service Center,
MSN 113; 127 Ninth Avenue, North; Nashville, TN 37234-0113;
by calling toll free (800) 458-2772; by faxing (615) 251-5933; by ordering
online at *www.lifeway.com*; by emailing *customerservice@lifeway.com*; or by
visiting a LifeWay Christian Store.

For information about adult discipleship and family resources, training, and
events, visit our Web site at *www.lifeway.com/discipleplus.*

Cover art: detail from the ceiling of the Sistine Chapel,
painted by Michelangelo

Printed in the United States of America

LifeWay Press
127 Ninth Avenue, North
Nashville, Tennessee 37234-0151

LifeWay.

*As God works through us, we will help people and churches
know Jesus Christ and seek His Kingdom by providing
biblical solutions that spiritually transform individuals and cultures.*

Contents

†he Au†hor

Rhonda Harrington Kelley has been called by God to minister to women. She came to know the Lord personally as a young girl and grew spiritually with the encouragement of her Christian parents, her Sunday School teachers, and her Girls in Action director. As a teenager Rhonda dedicated her life to special Christian service.

Rhonda grew up in New Orleans, Louisiana, where she graduated from John F. Kennedy High School. She received her B.A. and M.S. degrees in speech pathology and audiology from Baylor University.

In 1983 Rhonda earned a Ph.D. in special education/speech pathology from the University of New Orleans. Her career in speech pathology included clinical work in both hospital and private-practice settings. Rhonda served for 15 years as the director of the Division of Communicative Disorders at Ochsner Medical Institutions in New Orleans, Louisiana.

Rhonda and Charles S. (Chuck) Kelley, Jr., married in 1974 after dating for 4 years at Baylor University. Since 1975 they have lived in New Orleans, Louisiana, where Chuck serves as the president of New Orleans Baptist Theological Seminary. In addition to her responsibilities as the president's wife, Rhonda is a teacher, an author, a speaker, and a radio/TV host. The focus of her ministry has always been women. Women in the Bible have greatly influenced Rhonda's life. As a young girl she memorized Proverbs 31:10-31 and sought to become that godly woman. Her greatest desire is to equip women to develop a personal relationship with the Lord and live a godly lifestyle.

About This Study

*L*ife Lessons from Women in the Bible will give you opportunities to explore the lives of women in the Bible and to apply the lessons you learn to your life. This Bible study will be helpful to new Christians who want to begin studying God's Word, as well as to mature Christians who desire a deeper understanding of God's Word.

Life Lessons from Women in the Bible is a six-week, interactive Bible study with five daily lessons each week. Each week's study will focus on women of different ages and stages of life. Each day you will examine a specific woman in the Bible to learn a particular life lesson. While every life has many facets, you will examine only one specific life lesson from each Bible woman you study. The daily lessons, to be completed on your own, should take no more than 20 minutes. You will read about the woman from Scripture, learn about her culture, and meet her family. Learning activities focus on the woman's life and testimony and help you apply what you learn. Not all of the women are positive role models, so examine their actions by God's Word and learn from their mistakes. Esteem the godly women and follow their examples.

Following each week of individual study, you will gather with other women who are also studying this material. Small-group discussions will give you the opportunity to learn from the insights of others and will motivate you to learn more. Enlist a volunteer to lead the group discussion. A leader guide is provided on pages 91–95 of this book.

The introduction to each week's material suggests a life verse for the week—a Scripture that reinforces an important life lesson. Read this verse frequently during the week from several translations. Write it in your own words so that the verse becomes more meaningful to you. Try to memorize each life verse to hide God's Word in your heart and to apply it in your life. As you seek to live a godly life, allow each life verse to guide you and draw you to Him.

Week I
Women in the Bible

Overview of Week I
This week you will–
- learn about faith through the life of Ruth;
- see a picture of wisdom in the example of Abigail;
- glimpse hope in Christ through the story of Gomer;
- examine worship and service as demonstrated by Mary and Martha;
- experience the generosity of the faithful disciple Dorcas.

Women like You and Me
The Bible is truth. It records the stories of real people, including many interesting women. Woman is first mentioned in Genesis 2:22-23 when she was created by God, "taken out of man." Designed as man's counterpart, woman complements him in many ways. Created in God's image, woman has equal worth and value, as well as a unique role and function in God's plan.

The Bible mentions 187 women by name and includes hundreds of nameless women described as daughters, wives, mothers, widows, and so on. From these women of the Bible, women today can learn valuable lessons. Whether you are young or old, single or married, a mother or childless, a homemaker or a businesswoman, you can clearly see God's pattern for godly living in the lives of Old and New Testament women.

Many women in the Bible are best known for their relationships– whom they married or to whom they gave birth. Lessons about marriage and parenting can be learned from them. Other Bible women teach valuable life lessons about personal character and godly womanhood. Let's examine several Bible women as individuals to learn about Christian virtues. We can learn from these women of old because, after all, they were women like you and me.

This Week's Life Verse
"This woman was full of good works and charitable deeds which she did" (Acts 9:36).

7

This Week's Lessons
Day 1: Ruth: A Faithful Widow

Day 2: Abigail: A Wise Beauty

Day 3: Gomer: An Example of Hope

Day 4: Mary and Martha: Sisters Who Worshiped and Served

Day 5: Dorcas: A Generous Disciple

Day I

Ruth
A Faithful Widow

This Week's Life Verse

"This woman was full of good works and charitable deeds which she did" (Acts 9:36).

8

Today's Life Lesson
Faith

Today's Background Scripture
Ruth 1–4

The Old Testament Book of Ruth records the story of a young woman from Moab who chose by faith to follow the God of her mother-in-law, Naomi, instead of the gods of her ancestors. The Book of Ruth, named for its heroine, teaches many virtues of womanhood. While numerous life lessons can be learned from Ruth, abiding faith is her strongest legacy. Learn about faith from Ruth, a faithful widow.

Read today's background Scripture, Ruth 1–4.

Ruth's Legacy of Faith

Though a Gentile from Moab, Ruth became an ancestor of David and Jesus Christ (see Matt. 1:5-16). Ruth was born in Moab, the narrow strip of fertile land to the east of the Dead Sea. This well-watered area between the salty sea and a dry desert provided excellent conditions for farming and raising animals. The bounty of this land led Naomi and her family to Moab to escape the famine in Judah.

Ruth, whose name means *something worth seeing,* grew up worshiping other gods but later chose to follow the one true God. She married Mahlon, the Hebrew son of Naomi and Elimelech. Another son, Chilion, wedded a Moabitess named Orpah. After the deaths of all three men, Naomi decided to travel home to Judah. She encouraged her daughters-in-law to return to their families, but at that point Ruth chose by faith to follow Naomi.

Read Ruth 1:6-18 to examine Ruth's personal testimony of faith. How did Ruth demonstrate her faith?

_____

_____

What do you understand faith to be?

_____

_____

Hebrews 11:1 defines *faith* as "the substance of things hoped for, the evidence of things not seen." Ruth completely trusted in the God of Naomi, though she could not see Him and did not know her future. You can have that same kind of faith in a God who loves you and has a perfect plan for your life.

RUTH'S LIFE OF FAITH

Ruth's faith demanded action in her life. By faith she left her family in Moab and followed Naomi to Judah. She trusted God to provide for them and later married Boaz, her kinsman-redeemer. Ruth turned to God to know what to do, where to go, and whom to marry.

9

In chapter 2 Ruth meets Boaz, and in chapter 3 her future is secured. Review these chapters; then number the following events in the order of their occurrence.

_____ Boaz condoned Ruth's gleaning and provided her meals.

_____ Boaz married Ruth and fathered Obed, an ancestor of David.

_____ Ruth gleaned grain in the field of Boaz, Naomi's relative.

_____ Ruth appealed to Boaz as her kinsman-redeemer.

_____ Naomi proposed the plan for marriage (see Deut. 25:5-10).

In this great romance of the Old Testament, Ruth went to Boaz's field to pick up grain. Boaz, a relative of Naomi, condoned her gleaning in the field and provided her meals. Pleased with the meeting, Naomi proposed a plan that would lead to Ruth's marriage to Boaz. Ruth appealed to Boaz as her kinsman-redeemer. According to Jewish law, the nearest male relative was obliged to marry the widow of his relative (see Ruth 3:9-12; 4:7). Sometimes a correlation is made between the redemption of Ruth by Boaz and the redemption of sinners by Christ. (You should have numbered the events 2, 5, 1, 4, 3.)

Ruth lived her faith. As a result, God blessed her and her descendants. The rewards of her faith were without end. Her faith was a blessing to Naomi, who was cared for with love; to Boaz, her devoted husband and provider; and to her children and grandchildren, through whom the Messiah was born. Her faith is also a blessing to us today as recipients of God's gift of salvation through Jesus Christ.

Ruth's faith is a blessing to us today as recipients of God's gift of salvation through Jesus Christ.

RUTH'S LESSON OF FAITH

Although Ruth's family followed false gods, Ruth personally accepted the true God by faith because of the example of her mother-in-law, Naomi. Like Ruth, you must trust in the Lord for your own salvation.

When did you first profess faith in Jesus Christ?

_____

Think of women who have been godly examples in your life. Thank God for the influence they have had in your walk of faith.

I am grateful for my personal testimony of faith. As a six-year-old I chose to follow the God of my parents. While their lives of faith were powerful examples to me, I had to make a profession of faith for myself. In childlike faith I asked Jesus to come into my heart. My godly family nurtured my faith and challenged me to live my faith in my actions. I am grateful for the faithful women who have influenced my life, and I pray that God will use my life of faith to influence the women in my world.

Faith was available to the Gentiles of Moab as well as to the Jews of Judah (see Eph. 3:6). God graciously offers salvation to all through the blood of Jesus Christ. Faith is not inherited and is not exclusive. That's why Christians are commanded to share the gospel with all people.

When was the last time you shared with someone what Jesus Christ means to you?

_____

God provides for those who have faith in Him.

Ruth's faith was in God, not in herself or her circumstances. She was young, innocent, and weak. Her circumstances were tragic, hopeless, and insufficient, but God was the all-knowing, all-caring, all-sufficient Provider. God provides for those who have faith in Him.

How has God provided for you since you accepted Jesus by faith?

_____

_____

Ruth's faith demanded obedience. She followed God to Judah and to the field of Boaz. Her life of faith is an example to all believers. Faith must be lived in our actions, not just spoken with our lips.

How does your faith influence your actions?

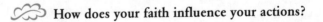

_____

The Lord blessed Ruth because of her faith. Her blessings overflowed to Naomi, Boaz, and Obed. In fact, through the lineage of David her blessings have been experienced by Christians throughout the ages. The Lord will reward your faithfulness, as well.

DAY 2

ABIGAIL

A WISE BEAUTY

Abigail was a beautiful, intelligent Hebrew woman trapped in a difficult marriage. Her husband, Nabal, was a wealthy, cruel descendant of Caleb. Though her husband didn't deserve her respect, Abigail was devoted to him. She saw his faults and loved him anyway. Abigail wisely committed herself to marriage, and she wisely counseled David at a crucial time.

 Read today's background Scripture, 1 Samuel 25:2-42.

A WISE WOMAN

Abigail, whose name means *my father rejoiced*, was the daughter of Nahash. She was later married by arrangement to Nabal, a wealthy landowner and shepherd. His name means *fool* or *rude and ill-bred*. The Scripture describes Abigail as both beautiful and wise. Unfortunately, she married a man who is not described as graciously.

 List the words used in 1 Samuel 25:3 to describe Abigail and Nabal.

Abigail: _____

Nabal: _____

Other verses in 1 Samuel 25 give additional descriptions of Nabal: selfish, unwilling to share (v. 11); immoral, unspiritual (v. 17); foolish, scoundrel (v. 25); drunk, glutton (v. 36). Abigail is described as wise, "a woman of good understanding" (1 Sam. 25:3). She wisely managed her household and saved the lives of her servants by giving David and his men food. She put her servants' security before her own safety. Her wise actions preserved both herself and her household.

A WISE WIFE

Though her husband acted foolishly, Abigail was wise. When Nabal refused David's request for food, Abigail intervened and delivered food to David and his men, averting his plan to kill Nabal. She wisely kept her actions a secret from her evil husband. Though she planned to tell Nabal of her actions later, she changed her mind when she found him drunk (see 1 Sam. 25:36). The next morning Abigail told her husband about David's plan to retaliate and her provision of food. The Bible says, "His heart died within him" (1 Sam. 25:37). He probably had a heart attack or a stroke, and he died 10 days later.

THIS WEEK'S
LIFE VERSE
"This woman was full of good works and charitable deeds which she did" (Acts 9:36).

TODAY'S LIFE LESSON
Wisdom

TODAY'S
BACKGROUND
SCRIPTURE
1 Samuel 25:2-42

11

Abigail wisely submitted to God's leadership and not to her husband's poor judgment.

Like many women today, Abigail found herself in a difficult marriage. Biblical instruction to wives is submission to husbands, but a believer must first be submissive to God. Nabal was an ungodly man whose defiant actions would have brought retaliation from David on his entire household. Abigail wisely submitted to God's leadership and not to her husband's poor judgment. Her actions were in the best interest of all, even selfish Nabal.

Read in 2 Samuel 14:2-24 the account of another wise woman David encountered.

The woman of Tekoa possessed unusual perception and dramatic persuasive ability. Her brilliant presentation, one of the finest speeches in the Bible (vv. 13-17), moved David to compassion. This wise woman tactfully convinced David to forgive Absalom and to call him back to Jerusalem.

A Wise Decision

Abigail's wisdom was also evident in her interaction with David. When Abigail delivered the food to him, she defused his anger with a humble confession and a generous gesture. She asked for forgiveness and praised his tolerance while arguing that it would be wrong to seek vengeance against her husband's household. Foreseeing the consequences of such needless bloodshed on his future leadership as king, Abigail was immensely wise in her approach with David.

First Samuel 25:29 contains an interesting Hebrew saying: " 'The life of my lord shall be bound in the bundle of the living with the Lord your God.' " These same words often mark Jewish tombstones, referring to life beyond the grave. The image comes from the custom of bundling valuable possessions to keep them from being broken. Abigail was saying that David was in God's bundle and was securely protected even though someone was pursuing him to take his life.[1]

David recognized Abigail's wisdom. After the death of her husband, Nabal, David married her (see 1 Sam. 25:39b-42). Of his eight wives, Abigail was certainly the most influential on his future leadership as king.

Wisdom is a gift of God. Describe a time when God gave you wisdom to offer help or to deal with a difficult situation.

_____

_____

Thank God for giving you wisdom. Pray that He will give you wisdom to face each day's circumstances.

DAY 3

GOMER
AN EXAMPLE OF HOPE

M any tragic situations seem hopeless. Many rebellious people seem beyond hope, but with God we can always have hope. The Bible contains accounts of circumstances and people with no hope in sight. God, in His sovereign power, intervenes and renews hope.

Gomer, the adulterous wife of the prophet Hosea, is a biblical example of a woman who seemed beyond hope. As you read about Gomer's return to God and her husband, Hosea, you will see a glimpse of God's unconditional love.

 Read today's background Scripture, Hosea 1–3.

HOPE IS BORN
In the land of Israel during the time of the Old Testament prophets, Hosea, a devoted servant of God, married Gomer, an immoral woman. Gomer, the daughter of Diblaim, is described as "a wife of harlotry" (Hos. 1:2). She gave birth to three children during her marriage to Hosea: Jezreel, Lo-Ruhamah, and Lo-Ammi. The hope of a fruitful ministry seemed to be dashed for the young preacher when his wife left him for an adulterous lifestyle. Hope for her own faith also seemed to falter when she turned her back on God and her marriage. Their children also followed the idolatrous life of their mother and became "children of harlotry" (Hos. 1:2).

 Gomer's sinful rebellion symbolized another situation in the Old Testament. Read Hosea 2:16,19-20. What do you understand to be the message of Hosea and Gomer's marriage?

_____

_____

Although their circumstances were real, Hosea and Gomer's situation also symbolized the adulterous life of the nation of Israel.

HOPE IS LOST
Hosea must have felt hopeless as Gomer lived a publicly immoral lifestyle. When his children rebelled against God, he must have been devastated.

**THIS WEEK'S
LIFE VERSE**
*"This woman was full of good
works and charitable deeds
which she did" (Acts 9:36).*

TODAY'S LIFE LESSON
Hope

**TODAY'S
BACKGROUND
SCRIPTURE**
Hosea 1–3

13

14

> Hosea 2 openly discusses the consequences of adultery. How does adultery harm a marriage relationship?

_____

_____

_____

To the people of Israel, this marriage had no hope. The godly prophet may have been counseled by concerned friends to divorce his sinful wife. That would certainly be common advice today.

> What does the Bible say about divorce when a spouse commits adultery? Read Deuteronomy 22:22 and Matthew 19:8-9.

_____

_____

_____

Mosaic law permitted divorce only in cases of infidelity, though later Jesus emphasized the permanence of marriage.

HOPE IS RESTORED

Because the prophet Hosea had faith in God, he did not give up on his marriage. How could he have hope in such a situation? His hope was based on God's unconditional love. Though it is difficult to have hope when facing life's challenges, God is the God of hope. Hope is best defined as *the certainty that God has something better for you.* With his faith in God, Hosea lived to see his marriage restored.

God told Hosea to marry Gomer, to bring her home, and to redeem her as his own. The marriage of Hosea and Gomer was restored. Hope was reborn, but the Lord gave specific terms for the reunion.

God is the God of hope.

> Read Hosea 3:3-5 and identify the terms of the reunion.

_____

_____

Hosea required Gomer to return to him, to their children, and to God. He expected her to live a godly life.

Reconciliation is a prominent theme in the Bible. God wants His children to be reconciled to Him and to one another.

Read the following passages. Then list the requirements for reconciliation to God and others.

Hosea 2:14-20: _____

_____

Jeremiah 3:13-14; 4:1-2: _____

_____

Romans 12:14-21: _____

_____

15

God wants His children to obey Him and to live in harmony with others, but human nature is sinful. Rebellion against God and ungodly behavior are natural to all people. The Bible reveals the only acceptable response to sin. Read 1 John 1:9 in the margin. Gomer discovered the joy of forgiveness and restoration through the Lord.

Do you have unconfessed sin in your life that is keeping you from enjoying a closer relationship with God? If so, write a prayer of repentance and pray it to Him.

_____

_____

_____

"If we confess our sins, He is faithful and just to forgive us our sins and to cleanse us from all unrighteousness" (1 John 1:9).

Is there a broken relationship in your life? Resolve to be reconciled with this person. Write what you need to do to bring about reconciliation.

_____

_____

_____

The Book of Hosea ends with a final call to repentance. When the sinful people turned from wickedness, Hosea's message and Gomer's life became ones of hope. Hope is available today even for those who have sinned against God.

DAY 4
MARY AND MARTHA
SISTERS WHO WORSHIPED AND SERVED

**THIS WEEK'S
LIFE VERSE**
*"This woman was full of good
works and charitable deeds
which she did" (Acts 9:36).*

**TODAY'S LIFE
LESSONS**
Worship and service

**TODAY'S
BACKGROUND
SCRIPTURES**
Luke 10:38-42
John 11:1-44; 12:1-8

16

The names of Mary and Martha are usually linked, but they were very different individuals. One was not better and the other worse. They were two women with different spiritual gifts and different personalities. While Mary worshiped Jesus, Martha served Him. While Mary sat sweetly, Martha bustled around the house. Yet both women had great spiritual insight in recognizing Jesus as the Messiah and sought to honor Him in their own ways.

Read today's background Scriptures, Luke 10:38-42; John 11:1-44; 12:1-8.

SISTERS WHO LOVED JESUS
Mary and Martha were born in Bethany, a town near Jerusalem, and were two of Jesus' most loved disciples. He often visited in the home of Martha; Mary; and their brother, Lazarus. You have read the accounts of the three encounters between Jesus and these sisters.

Review Luke 10:38-42. How did Martha serve Jesus?

_____

How did Mary worship Jesus?

_____

Both women loved the Lord, but they expressed their love in different ways. Martha had the spiritual gift of service, and Mary had the gift of worship. Martha warmly welcomed Jesus and began preparing food for the guests, while Mary sat at Jesus' feet, hungry to hear His teachings. When Martha complained that Mary was not helping her with the meal, Jesus reminded Martha of eternal matters and encouraged her to affirm Mary: " 'Martha, Martha, you are worried and troubled about many things. But one thing is needed, and Mary has chosen that good part, which will not be taken away from her' " (Luke 10:41-42). Although Jesus did not condemn Martha's unselfish service, He praised Mary's loving worship. He reminded Martha of the most important priority: to love and worship Him.

Think about your service for the Lord. Are you so busy serving that you don't have time to worship Him? On the next page write ways you can worship God in addition to serving Him.

_____

_____

John 11:1-44 gives the account of the death of the sisters' brother, Lazarus. The sisters sent for Jesus when Lazarus got sick, but he had died by the time Jesus reached Bethany. As Jesus talked with Martha, she declared, " 'I believe that You are the Christ, the Son of God, who is to come into the world' " (John 11:27). It is clear that Martha recognized Jesus as the Messiah.

17

The final encounter is recorded in John 12:1-8. Again Martha was serving others, having prepared dinner for Jesus and His disciples. While Martha served, Mary anointed Jesus' feet with expensive perfume and wiped His feet with her hair. This act revealed that Mary also recognized Jesus as the Messiah. We read in the Matthew acccount of this incident that Jesus praised Mary's act of honor in preparation for his death and burial. Read His words in the margin.

Different Gifts, One Lord

Mary and Martha loved the same Lord and used their different spiritual gifts of worship and service for His glory. My sister, Mitzi, and I love and serve the same Lord, although we have different gifts and personalities. During our teenage years I often thought of myself as a Martha and of my sister as a Mary. It seemed that I was always in the kitchen helping my mother serve the food while Mitzi was in the dining room talking with guests. Like Martha, I often complained to my mother that my sister had left me to do the work alone, although I never had the nerve to complain to the Lord! Wisely, my mother reminded me of the importance of Christian fellowship and suggested that I refocus my priorities.

" 'Assuredly, I say to you, wherever this gospel is preached in the whole world, what this woman has done will also be told as a memorial to her' " (Matt. 26:13).

God has called many to serve Him. He chooses to work through all believers who serve Him unselfishly with their spiritual gifts. No matter what your spiritual gift is, use it selflessly to bring glory and honor to God, as Mary and Martha used their different gifts to honor the Lord. They are wonderful examples for Christian women today.

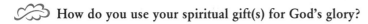 How do you use your spiritual gift(s) for God's glory?

_____

_____

Whether or not you have the spiritual gift of service like Martha, you can serve others in Christ's name. Name ways you will do this.

_____

DAY 5
DORCAS
A GENEROUS DISCIPLE

THIS WEEK'S LIFE VERSE
"This woman was full of good works and charitable deeds which she did" (Acts 9:36).

18

TODAY'S LIFE LESSON
Generosity

TODAY'S BACKGROUND SCRIPTURE
Acts 9:36-42

L ittle is known of Dorcas's personal background. She lived among Greeks in the first century in Joppa, a city located about 40 miles west of Jerusalem along the Mediterranean coast in Israel. While her Greek name was Dorcas, her Aramaic name was Tabitha. Both names are mentioned in Scripture. Dorcas was named for the gazelle, a small, swift animal that symbolized beauty in the Middle East. This disciple of Joppa is not known to have a husband or children. She is known for only one thing—her "good works and charitable deeds" (Acts 9:36). What a great reputation to be known as a generous disciple!

🌥 **Read today's background Scripture, Acts 9:36-42.**

A GENEROUS SPIRIT
Unselfish generosity is not a common quality. In fact, most children are innately selfish and stingy. The early vocabulary of young children includes words like *me, my,* and *mine.* A child's world is self-centered and self-seeking. People have a strong natural desire to accumulate more for self. They must be taught to give to others and share.

Dorcas was a very generous, giving person. Though she had little, she shared what she had with others who had greater need. As a result, she was deeply loved and appreciated.

🌥 **In Acts 9:36-42 what words indicate Dorcas's generosity to others?**

_____

_____

Another generous disciple mentioned in Scripture is the widow with two mites (see Mark 12:41-44; Luke 21:1-4). Though she had only two small coins, she didn't hoard them for herself. She gave them graciously and without a show. Her humble generosity is a testimony to all believers.

🌥 **Do you know some generous givers? unselfish saints? As you write their names, thank God for giving them generous spirits.**

_____

Pray that God will give you a generous spirit like the one reflected in these words by David Livingstone: "I will place no value on anything I may possess except in relation to the Kingdom of Christ. If anything I have will advance the interests of that Kingdom, it shall be given away or kept, only as by giving or keeping it I may promote the glory of Him, to whom I owe all my hopes in time and eternity."[2]

GENEROUS GESTURES

It is one thing to want to give and another thing to actually give. Dorcas had a generous spirit that led to generous gestures. Acts 9 reveals a practical response to tangible needs. Widows in Joppa needed clothes. Dorcas used her creative ability as a seamstress to make garments for the widows. She gave generously from love.

God has made specific provision for widows. The New Testament teaches that God's people are to honor, provide for, and care for the widows among them (see 1 Tim. 5:3-16). Believers' generosity is part of God's plan for the care of widows.

What does your church do to minister to the widows of your congregation?

_____

_____

In some churches the deacons assume responsibility for the care of widows. In other churches Bible-study groups minister to widows. One church sponsors a widow's tea every Christmas to honor faithful women who have lost their husbands and to provide an opportunity for fellowship. Church bodies as a whole or an individual believer like Dorcas can reach out in love to those in need.

The Old Testament describes another widow who was cared for by the generosity of others. Read 1 Kings 17:8-16 and discover how the widow of Zarephath trusted God for her provision. God used the prophet Elijah to promise sustenance. Scripture says that the widow and her household had enough food to eat for many days. Be sensitive to the needs of people around you and respond with generous gestures.

List ways you can be more generous in giving to others in need.

_____

_____

19

Be sensitive to the needs of people around you and respond with generous gestures.

Generous Blessings

The Bible teaches generosity in giving, but it also teaches generosity in receiving. A godly Christian not only gives sacrificially but also receives abundant blessings. Isn't that just like God? He doesn't ask of us anything He hasn't already given. After all, God is the giver of all things. He has blessed us abundantly.

Name ways God has blessed you and your family.

_____

_____

_____

_____

Stop and thank God for His abundant blessings.

Dorcas was blessed abundantly by her generous giving. The widows returned her generosity with love, gratitude, and respect. At her death they were filled with grief. As they testified of her generosity, Peter was deeply moved. God used Peter to restore life to Dorcas, an act that drew attention to God's power and led many to believe in Christ. Further blessings resulted for the widows and for all believers!

Paul reminds us in Ephesians 3 that God blesses us more abundantly than we could ever ask or think. Dorcas lived a life of generosity to others and experienced God's abundant blessings. Follow Dorcas's example and give to others as God has given to you.

Give to others as God has given to you.

---

[1] Dorothy Kelley Patterson and Rhonda Harrington Kelley, eds., *The Woman's Study Bible* (Nashville: Thomas Nelson Publishers, 1995), 487.

[2] David Livingstone, as quoted by Gien Karssen, *Her Name Is Woman* (Colorado Springs: Navpress, 1975), 155.

WEEK 2
WIVES IN THE BIBLE

OVERVIEW OF WEEK 2
This week you will–
- see a picture of biblical submission in Sarah;
- learn about kindness from the maiden Rebekah;
- understand true love through the trials of Rachel;
- study the importance of affirmation in the example of Elizabeth;
- examine the role of companionship in the marriage of Sapphira.

A WIFE IS A GOOD THING
While many women in the Bible are best known for the men they married, each woman has a personal identity and an independent life. Each woman is loved and valued by God, but many women develop their fullest potential in the marriage relationship. Married women in the Bible can teach married women today how to love their husbands. If you are not married, these biblical examples can teach you how to practice godly virtues in other relationships and how to submit to God, love Him, and be faithful to Him.

Many women in the Bible were married. Both the Old and New Testaments teach that the marriage commitment is to be second in importance only to commitment to God. Marriage was instituted by God (see Gen. 2:24) and is illustrated in the relationship of Jesus to His bride, the church (see Eph. 5:23-27). Marriage was intended to last for a lifetime and to strengthen each partner through the union.

While many wives are named in Scripture, the names of some were not recorded:
- Cain's wife (see Gen. 4:17)
- Noah's wife (see Gen. 6:18; 7:7,13; 8:16,18)
- Lot's wife (see Gen. 19:26; Luke 17:32)
- Potiphar's wife (see Gen. 39:7-9,12,19)
- Samson's wife (see Judg. 14:15-16,20; 15:6)
- Job's wife (see Job 2:9; 19:17; 31:10)
- Peter's wife (see Matt. 8:14; Mark 1:30; Luke 4:38; 1 Cor. 9:5)
- Pilate's wife (see Matt. 27:19)

At times you may feel unimportant or inconsequential when introduced as someone's wife. But remember what is said in Proverbs 18:22: "He who finds a wife finds a good thing." A wife is a good thing! Let's learn from these wives in the Bible how to be a good wife.

THIS WEEK'S LIFE VERSE
" 'Blessed are you among women, and blessed is the fruit of your womb!' " (Luke 1:42).

21

THIS WEEK'S LESSONS
Day 1: Sarah: A Submissive Woman
Day 2: Rebekah: A Kind Bride
Day 3: Rachel: A Loving Beauty
Day 4: Elizabeth: An Affirming Wife
Day 5: Sapphira: An Agreeable Companion

DAY 1

SARAH
A SUBMISSIVE WOMAN

**THIS WEEK'S
LIFE VERSE**
*" 'Blessed are you among
women, and blessed is the fruit
of your womb!' " (Luke 1:42).*

TODAY'S LIFE LESSON
Submission

**TODAY'S
BACKGROUND
SCRIPTURES**
Genesis 11:29–12:20; 16;
23:1-2

More space is devoted to Sarah than to any other woman in the Bible. She is heralded as a wife, a mother, and a paragon of faith. Sarah is mentioned several times in the New Testament. Romans 4:19 and 9:9 refer to Sarah's infertility and to God's miraculous provision of a child. In Galatians 4:21-31 Sarah is chosen to illustrate the difference between the bondage of the law and freedom through Jesus Christ. And in 1 Peter 3:5-6 Sarah is commended for her obedience to God and to Abraham. Sarah is the only wife named with the heroes of the faith in Hebrews 11 (see v. 11). Her godly life remains a testimony of faithful submission for all Christian women today.

Read today's background Scriptures, Genesis 11:29–12:20; 16; 23:1-2.

A SUBMISSIVE FOLLOWER

Sarah was born in Ur of the Chaldeans, the daughter of Terah, who worshiped idols (see Josh. 24:2). At first she was called Sarai, which means *to contend*, but her name was changed to Sarah (*princess*) when she was 90 years old. God gave her a new name as a sign of His covenant to bring about a new nation through her womb (see Gen. 17:15-16). She was married to her half-brother, Abraham, and traveled north with his family to Haran in Canaan. Marriage between brothers and sisters was necessary at that time, though later family unions were forbidden as incestuous (see Lev. 18).

Scripture first records Sarah's submission to Abraham when she followed her husband to Canaan and Egypt. She then submitted to his plan to conceal their marriage from Pharaoh. Believing Sarah's beauty to be desired by Pharaoh, Abraham feared for his life and asked Sarah to say that she was his sister. She was taken to Pharaoh's house, and Abraham was treated well. But eventually, Pharaoh learned about their marriage and sent Sarah away.

Submission to authority often requires a wife to follow the husband's leadership even to unknown destinations. God blessed Sarah's obedience to Him and her submission to Abraham. A wife's submission is not only to her husband but also to God and His plan for their marriage.

If you are married, seek to be submissive like Sarah. I struggled with submission as a young wife. I was an independent person, a strong-minded woman. And though I still am, I have come to understand why and how God wants me to submit to my husband's leadership.

It is God's divine plan for marriage. As I submit my own will to God, it becomes easier for me to submit to my husband. I submit myself to him as to the Lord. I experience great joy in obedient submission, and God commands my husband to love me with all his heart.

Rate the way you feel about submission to your husband by marking your attitude on the following continuum.

A major problem   It depends   No problem

23

Why did you answer the way you did? _____

_____

If submission is difficult for you, read Ephesians 5:22-33 and commit to pray about this issue.

A MANIPULATIVE FOLLOWER

Submissive Sarah became impatient as she waited on the Lord to give her a child. Like many impatient, self-sufficient believers today, she decided to take matters into her own hands. She chose to interfere in God's plan, to manipulate His will.

Reread Sarah's plan in Genesis 16. What effect did her actions have on—

herself? _____

Hagar and Ishmael? _____

Abraham? _____

their children to come? _____

God gave Abraham a son by Hagar (Ishmael) and, as promised, a son by Sarah (Isaac). Sarah began to hate Hagar and Ishmael as obvious reminders of her disobedience and lack of faith. Hagar and Ishmael were sent away, but Ishmael later became a father of nations. Sarah's sin and selfishness bore grave consequences, but God restored her relationship with Him. Her faith was renewed, and she resumed her roles as a submissive wife and a follower of God.

Today many women face the heartbreak of infertility. Most couples anticipate children after marriage, and some are disappointed when children don't arrive. Though Christian women may have a strong desire for parenthood, it is most important to submit to God's will for

> Sarah chose to interfere in God's plan, to manipulate His will.

that union. Some couples pursue fertility treatment. Others choose adoption, while some couples remain childless. Peace always lies in knowing God's will for each family. Manipulating God's plan always carries great risks.

 Think of a time when you manipulated God's plan. What were the consequences?

_____

_____

Ask God to teach you to submit to His will without fear.

A Repentant Follower

The facts that Sarah's death was greatly mourned by her godly husband (see Gen. 23:1-2) and that she was remembered as one of the faithful (see Heb. 11:11) indicate that Sarah lived a holy life in her later years. Having died at the age of 127 in the land of Canaan, she was buried in a cave in the field of Machpelah.

Like many Christian women today, Sarah experienced the blessings of submission and the consequences of disobedience. When she rebelled against God's authority, her life was shattered. When she repented of her rebellion and submitted to God's authority, Sarah was blessed beyond her wildest imagination. Women today can learn about real-life submission from this strong-willed wife.

Many times when we cannot submit to others, we also have difficulty submitting to God. As you proceed through this study, pray that God will show His will to you and that you will submit to what He reveals.

Day 2

REBEKAH
A Kind Bride

This Week's Life Verse
" 'Blessed are you among women, and blessed is the fruit of your womb!' " (Luke 1:42).

Today's Life Lesson
Kindness

Kindness is a virtue, a fruit of the Holy Spirit evidenced in a believer's life. In both the Old and New Testaments kindness refers to steadfast love expressed in actions. The Lord Himself is kind (see Ps. 31:21), and He wants His children to be kind (see Eph. 4:32). Kindness is reflected in both words and deeds.

Rebekah showed kindness to strangers when she gave water to Abraham's servant, Eliezer, and his camels. Rebekah's kindness paved the way for her marriage to Isaac, but later in life her kindness faltered. Her kindness makes Rebekah a positive role model for women today, while her failures direct Christian women to the everlasting kindness of the Lord.

25

Read today's background Scriptures, Genesis 24:10-27, 58-67; 25:19-27,46; 27.

A KIND MAIDEN

Rebekah, the daughter of Bethuel and great-niece of Abraham, was a beautiful young virgin living in Haran. As usual, she went to the well for water at the end of the day, unaware that an encounter with a stranger would alter her future. Eliezer, Abraham's trusted servant, had traveled to Haran in search of a godly wife for Isaac. Rebekah's kind actions identified her as Isaac's intended mate, and she returned to Canaan to marry him.

Genesis 24:58-67 describes the meeting and subsequent marriage of Isaac and Rebekah. When Isaac heard about Rebekah's kindness to Eliezer, he knew that Rebekah was God's appointed one for him. Their marriage vows were sealed when Isaac took Rebekah to the tent of his mother, Sarah. Later, Rebekah's kindness to Isaac comforted him after his mother's death. Kindness is an attractive quality!

A KIND WIFE

Rebekah and Isaac's marriage was the first monogamous one on record. Little is known about the early years of their marriage, but we can imagine that her love and kindness were reciprocated by her adoring husband. For 20 years Isaac and Rebekah experienced the affluence of Abraham's inheritance.

Though blessed with love, Rebekah's life was not blessed with children. Isaac pleaded with the Lord for his barren wife to have a child. Like Sarah, Rebekah faced the helpless problem of infertility. Barrenness in the Old Testament world was regarded as the effects of sin in a fallen world and the withdrawal of God's blessing on a couple.

Today many couples face the dilemma of infertility. They are challenged to seek God's will for children and to remain joyful in marriage despite disappointment.

Do you know women today who deal with infertility? Write their names here and pray that God will comfort them and will assure them of His blessings on their marriage.

My husband and I faced the challenge of infertility a few years after we were married. When we first learned of our inability to conceive children, we were disappointed and confused. After carefully considering our options, we decided to abandon our dream for children. Yet God has given us a ministry to children. In fact, our quiver is full (see Ps. 127:5), since we consider ourselves the parents of the faculty, staff, and students of the seminary of which my husband is the president. God has blessed us with more children than we ever dreamed of!

Numerous women in the Bible did not bear children. However, they were influential in others' lives. Despite disappointment, childless women must continue to love and cherish their husbands. Though anger and bitterness can overflow from disappointment, Christian wives must show kindness to their husbands throughout marriage. Kindness in marriage is a testimony of God's grace.

 How do you demonstrate kindness in your marriage?

_____

_____

Commit to show your husband kindness each day.

A Kind Mother

After 20 years of barrenness Rebekah gave birth to twins, Esau and Jacob. Even their birth revealed a sign of the brothers' future struggle. The secondborn, Jacob, held Esau's heel, foreshadowing the later fighting between the Edomite nation and Israel. The brothers' jealousy was encouraged by Rebekah's deceit when she convinced Jacob to trick his feeble father into giving him Esau's inheritance. Rebekah's extreme kindness toward Jacob caused her to be unmercifully cruel to Esau.

How did Esau respond to the deceit of his mother and his brother? Read Genesis 27:34-41. Record Esau's feelings here.

_____

Kindness, the strength of Rebekah's character, became her greatest weakness when carried to the extreme. Because Rebekah loved Jacob too much, she showered love and affection on him. This favoritism harmed Rebekah's relationship with Isaac, whom she deceived. It is as important for a woman to show love and kindness to her husband as to her children.

Has your kindness ever gotten out of balance? What were the consequences?

_____

26

Kindness in marriage is a testimony of God's grace.

Ask God for forgiveness; then seek to be kind to all.

Genesis 27:46 records these revealing words by Rebekah later in life: " 'I am weary of my life.' " When a kind person becomes hateful and vindictive, joy ends. Surely Rebekah never intended to become an unkind wife and mother. But by the time of her death she had experienced a long separation from her beloved son Jacob. Rebekah's life is a strong example of the need for impartial kindness.

DAY 3

RACHEL
A LOVING BEAUTY

Beauty may be the first quality to attract a man to a woman, but outward appearance is only skin deep. Inner beauty is the virtue that matters to God and that sustains a relationship. The Scripture describes many women as beautiful–Sarah (see Gen. 12:11), Rebekah (see Gen. 24:16), Abigail (see 1 Sam. 25:3), Bathsheba (see 2 Sam. 11:2), and Rachel (see Gen. 29:17). However, the Bible most often praises a woman's heart. True beauty comes from within and is reflected in the countenance. First Peter 3:3-4 states, "Do not let your adornment be merely outward ... rather let it be the hidden person of the heart, with the incorruptible beauty of a gentle and quiet spirit, which is very precious in the sight of God." Rachel was a love-filled beauty in the sight of God and others.

Read today's background Scriptures, Genesis 29:6-35; 30:22-24; 35:16-20.

A HEBREW BEAUTY

Rachel, whose name means *ewe,* was the youngest daughter of Laban, Jacob's uncle in Haran, Mesopotamia. One day while watering her father's sheep, she met Jacob, the son of Isaac and grandson of Abraham, when he was fleeing from his brother, Esau, whom he had betrayed. When Jacob saw Rachel, it must have been love at first sight.

The Bible says that "Rachel was beautiful of form and appearance" (Gen. 29:17). Read Genesis 29:10-12 and describe Jacob's response when he saw Rachel.

_____

Jacob immediately fell in love with the Hebrew beauty Rachel.

THIS WEEK'S LIFE VERSE
" *'Blessed are you among women, and blessed is the fruit of your womb!' "* (Luke 1:42).

TODAY'S LIFE LESSON
Love

TODAY'S BACKGROUND SCRIPTURES
Genesis 29:6-35; 30:22-24; 35:16-20

28

AN AWAITED WIFE

Jacob wanted to marry Rachel, but ancient Near Eastern custom demanded a bride-price to be paid to the bride's parents. He offered to work seven years to marry Rachel, Laban's younger daughter. A covenant agreement was made between Jacob and Laban for the hand of Rachel in marriage. Covenant relationships are an integral part of Scripture and an important bond in God's relationship with people. Simply stated, a covenant is an agreement between two parties. God is a covenant-maker who desires a covenant relationship with His people. God's covenants are not to be broken.

Read these Scriptures and identify the person in covenant with God.

Genesis 9:1-17: _____

Genesis 17:1-22: _____

Genesis 26:3-5: _____

Genesis 28:13-22: _____

Exodus 19:5-6: _____

Psalm 89:3-4,28,34: _____

> The ultimate covenant was made by God with humanity through Jesus Christ's death on the cross.

Covenants were made in the Old and New Testaments, but the ultimate covenant was made by God with humanity through Jesus Christ's death on the cross.

Jacob fulfilled his covenant with Laban by working for seven years, but Laban didn't honor his covenant. Instead, he gave his elder daughter, Leah, to Jacob in marriage. The irony of this story is that Jacob was tricked into marrying Leah, who had weak eyes, just as Jacob himself had tricked his father, Isaac, who had failing eyesight (see Gen. 27:18-29).

How Jacob must have loved Rachel! He worked for seven more years to marry her. Rachel must have loved Jacob, too, because she patiently waited to become his bride.

The right spouse is worth waiting for—and worth praying for! Think of a young woman who is waiting for the right person and commit to pray for this woman regularly. If you have children, begin now making this important life decision a matter of prayer.

A LOVING PARTNER

The marriage between Jacob and Rachel experienced many highs and lows. While their love bound them together through the years, their life together was always in turmoil. Leah and Rachel were extremely jealous of each other. Rachel was unable to conceive a child for Jacob and remained angry at her father, Laban, for his deceit. She worshiped other gods and later fled with Jacob to Gilead (see Gen. 31:21).

Rachel finally became pregnant and gave birth to Joseph, Jacob's favorite son. In her later years she gave birth to a second son, Benjamin, and then she died. Rachel's death during childbirth was no great surprise since she had cried out for death in her desperation to have children (see Gen. 30:1).

29

Rachel was a woman who loved deeply. She loved her husband, Jacob, and she loved her sons. Yet her love did not protect her from deep sorrow. Is love presently causing sorrow and turmoil for you? Rachel cried out for death in her desperation. Cry out to God not for death but for His provision in your need. Write your prayer to Him.

Rachel's love did not protect her from deep sorrow.

_____

_____

_____

_____

_____

_____

Rachel is remembered in Scripture outside this Genesis account. Read these passages about Rachel:

"The Lord make the woman who is coming to your house like Rachel and Leah, the two who built the house of Israel" (Ruth 4:11).

"A voice was heard in Ramah,
Lamentation and bitter weeping,
Rachel weeping for her children,
refusing to be comforted for her children" (Jer. 31:15).

Rachel, Jacob's second wife, loved her husband. Despite her flaws, she gave the world outstanding sons and exemplified a life of love. She was an honored daughter of Yahweh.

ELIZABETH
AN AFFIRMING WIFE

**THIS WEEK'S
LIFE VERSE**
" *'Blessed are you among
women, and blessed is the fruit
of your womb!'* " *(Luke 1:42).*

30

TODAY'S LIFE LESSON
Affirmation

**TODAY'S
BACKGROUND
SCRIPTURE**
Luke 1:5-66

Words of affirmation and praise are gifts to the hearer. In all relationships, including marriage, affirmation is a balm. In fact, Willard F. Harley, Jr., says that affirmation is not only desired but also needed. Admiration is one of the five most basic needs of men in marriage.[1] Husbands need to be praised by their wives, especially in a world that criticizes and discourages.

In the New Testament Paul teaches the importance of affirmation or encouragement. Every word spoken should build up: "Let no corrupt word proceed out of your mouth, but what is good for necessary edification, that it may impart grace to the hearers" (Eph. 4:29). Encouragement or edification is a spiritual gift to be used as a ministry to others. Elizabeth received God's praise, and through her godly life she offered praise to others and to God. She was a true encourager—an affirming woman, wife, and mother.

Read today's background Scripture, Luke 1:5-66.

PRAISE FROM GOD

Luke described Elizabeth as a woman who was "righteous before God, walking in all the commandments and ordinances of the Lord blameless" (Luke 1:6). Elizabeth was descended from a priest, Aaron, and married a priest, Zacharias. She lived in the country of Judea near Jerusalem, where her husband served as priest in the temple. Her name means *my God is good fortune* or *my God has sworn an oath.* She was a godly wife, honoring her husband's role of religious leadership. As a result, she was blessed by God.

God praised Elizabeth's righteous life and blessed her barrenness with a child. An angel appeared to Zacharias to announce the birth of a son. The birth announcements of John the Baptist and Jesus Christ are very similar.

Read the two birth announcements in Luke 1:11-22 and Luke 1:26-38. Then list four similarities below.

1. _____

2. _____

3. _____

4. _____

Angels announced the births of John the Baptist and Jesus. Both births were unusual, involving the work of the Holy Spirit. Both newborns were to be sons, in fulfillment of Old Testament prophecies. Both sons were to be part of God's plan to save a lost world.

Elizabeth and her husband, Zacharias, were blessed with a child of prophecy. They parented a son who was the forerunner of Jesus Christ, the Messiah. Their godly lives brought them tremendous blessings from God.

PRAISE OF OTHERS

Elizabeth had influence as a wife and a mother. She also had influence as a friend and a mentor. She was a relative of Mary of Nazareth, who became the mother of Jesus. Both women were pregnant for the first time, and they developed a strong bond of friendship. They shared a devotion to God and a love for each other.

The older woman, Elizabeth, became a spiritual mentor to the younger woman, Mary. Through her daily example and constant encouragement Elizabeth influenced young Mary.

Mentoring relationships promote spiritual growth in women. Who have been some influential mentors in your life?

_____

_____

In her book *A Garden Path to Mentoring* Esther Burroughs says that mentoring is "pouring your love for God into another. They will begin to see His mission for their lives and, hopefully, will become obedient to His missions call."[2] In the Scriptures older women are challenged to teach younger, less experienced women (see Titus 2: 1-5). God ordained mentoring as a ministry to others and as a blessing to women.

Elizabeth offered great affirmation and praise to Mary when she proclaimed, " 'Blessed are you among women, and blessed is the fruit of your womb!' " (Luke 1:42). Then she added, " 'Blessed is she who believed, for there will be a fulfillment of those things which were told her from the Lord' " (Luke 1:45). Elizabeth's faith was an example to Mary. God blesses us, like Mary, with mentors who teach and affirm us. Like Elizabeth, we need to mentor and encourage others.

Have you thought about mentoring another woman? Name several possibilities and begin praying about this opportunity to influence someone's spiritual growth and to offer affirmation.

_____

> God ordained mentoring as a ministry to others and as a blessing to women.

32

Praise from Others

Jesus Christ Himself gave Elizabeth her greatest praise when He said, " 'Assuredly, I say to you, among those born of women there has not risen one greater than John the Baptist' " (Matt. 11:11). John the Baptist, himself a great prophet, prepared the way for the Messiah's ministry. He preached repentance and judgment and lived a very simple, rugged lifestyle. The significance of his ministry was confirmed when he baptized Jesus in the Jordan River (see Mark 1: 9-11). Jesus praised Elizabeth's life because she had raised a godly son.

As Elizabeth and Mary awaited their sons' births, neither fully understood the impact on history their sons would make. Nor could either woman have been aware of the cruel deaths their sons would face. After a very popular ministry (see Matt. 21:31-32; Mark 11: 27-32; Luke 7:29-30; John 10:41) John the Baptist was imprisoned and then beheaded. (The account of his death is found in Mark 6:14-29.) Jesus Christ, the Savior of the world, was crucified on a cross after a very brief three-year ministry. (Jesus' crucifixion is recorded in Mark 15:20-37.) For Elizabeth and Mary the miraculous births of their sons were causes for joyous celebration; their deaths were painful but powerful components of God's plan for the redemption of the world.

We know that Elizabeth and Mary affirmed each other. How do you think the women could have comforted each other after the tragic deaths of their sons? Write a note of encouragement from one to the other.

_____

_____

_____

_____

_____

_____

God selected Elizabeth for a special role in His plan to bring redemption to humankind.

God selected Elizabeth for a special role in His plan to bring redemption to humankind. As a result, she had God-given opportunities to affirm and encourage Mary, the mother of our Savior, Jesus Christ. Today's women can also have an influence as they mentor other women and encourage them in their spiritual growth.

DAY 5

SAPPHIRA
AN AGREEABLE COMPANION

ompanionship, or the company of another, provides both encouragement and joy. Recreational companionship is a man's second most basic need in marriage.[3] Husbands want to spend time with their wives sharing a favorite activity. Being together builds the marriage relationship, fosters intimacy, and provides opportunities for communication. Sapphira, a wife in the New Testament, and her husband, Ananias, spent time together. These companions were devoted to each other. However, as we will see, devotion is empty if a couple is not also devoted to God.

**THIS WEEK'S
LIFE VERSE**
" 'Blessed are you among women, and blessed is the fruit of your womb!' " (Luke 1:42).

TODAY'S LIFE LESSON
Companionship

TODAY'S BACKGROUND SCRIPTURE
Acts 5:1-10

33

Read today's background Scripture, Acts 5:1-10.

COMPANIONS IN DEVOTION

Sapphira and her husband, Ananias, were active members of the early church in Jerusalem. Together they allied themselves with the disciples in building the kingdom of God here on earth. They may have witnessed Jesus' ministry personally, and they may have been two of the thousands saved at Pentecost. They certainly experienced many great works of the Holy Spirit (see Acts 2–4). During their time the apostles Peter and John were preaching evangelistically. The church was experiencing explosive growth, and miraculous healings were being performed. Though Ananias and Sapphira watched the work of the Holy Spirit, they didn't completely understand His power.

Read the following Scriptures and draw lines across the columns to identify the roles of the Holy Spirit in the lives of believers.

John 16:8	Empowers us for service
John 16:13	Directs us
Acts 1:8	Convicts us of sin
Romans 8:14	Helps us pray
Romans 8:26	Guides us into truth

The Holy Spirit is the third person of the Trinity who convicts us of sin (see John 16:8), guides us into truth (see John 16:13), empowers us for service (see Acts 1:8), directs us (see Rom. 8:14), and helps us pray (see Rom. 8:26). The Holy Spirit forms a partnership with the believer that lasts through eternity. Sapphira enjoyed companionship with God through the Holy Spirit's presence and companionship with Ananias through their partnership in marriage and ministry.

34

🌥 In addition to companionship as a couple, do you and your husband enjoy companionship with God? Begin or renew your commitment to a regular time of Bible study and prayer together.

COMPANIONS IN DECEIT

Ananias and Sapphira are remembered by most Bible readers for their overwhelming sin. Although they serve as a negative example, they can challenge Christian couples to be godly companions in marriage. Partners in the work of the church, Sapphira and Ananias became partners in deceit. After selling some property, they selfishly kept some of the proceeds from the church. When questioned by Peter, each lied about the profits and denied any deception. While Ananias and Sapphira remained committed to each other, they forgot their devotion to God.

🌥 Have you been a negative influence in the life of another person or led someone into sin? If so, confess that sin to God and ask forgiveness of the one you led to stumble. Pray, renewing your commitment to live a righteous life.

COMPANIONS IN DEATH

Greed and deceit became the downfall of Sapphira and Ananias. A marriage that began in devotion to God ended in the deceit of His church. Their marriage and ministry were undoubtedly strengthened by their unified efforts, but their deaths were brought about by their dishonest schemes. Their lives may be an example of companionship taken to the extreme!

The Holy Spirit punished Ananias and Sapphira's sin with death. When Ananias lied to Peter about the amount of profit he had given, he was struck dead. The equally guilty Sapphira met the same fate. When she lied to the Holy Spirit and to the church leaders, she immediately died.

🌥 Take a minute to examine what Scripture teaches about sin. Read the Scriptures in the margin. Then thank God for His forgiveness of your sin. Pledge to flee from sin.

Companionship in marriage is important, but it can become misguided, meaningless, and even disastrous if the couple does not submit to the lordship of Christ. As a couple, commit yourself to God and pledge to be godly companions to each other.

" 'Be sure your sin will find you out' " (Num. 32:23).

"My sin is always before me" (Ps. 51:3).

" 'Behold, the Lamb of God who takes away the sin of the world!' " (John 1:29).

"The wages of sin is death" (Rom. 6:23).

"If we confess our sins, He is faithful and just to forgive us our sins" (1 John 1:9).

[1]Willard F. Harley, Jr., *His Needs, Her Needs* (Tarrytown, NY: Fleming H. Revell Company, 1986), 10.
[2]Esther Burroughs, *A Garden Path to Mentoring* (Birmingham, AL: New Hope, 1997), 7.
[3]Harley, *His Needs, Her Needs,* 10.

WEEK 3
MOTHERS IN THE BIBLE

OVERVIEW OF WEEK 3

This week you will–
- witness God's grace in Eve's life;
- learn about devotion from Hannah;
- discover the importance of influence through the life of Naomi;
- examine the tenderness of Mary, the mother of Jesus;
- consider the nature of maternal nurturing in Lois and Eunice.

MOTHERHOOD IS A GREAT CALLING

Most women who rear children would agree that motherhood is a great calling. When God chooses to give a child by birth or adoption, a woman is blessed beyond measure. The Bible includes the stories of many mothers, women who influenced their children for good or evil. Many are named, while others are simply described as mothers. From Scripture mothers today can receive encouragement, guidance, and specific tips for parenting. Women who are not mothers can use these lessons to influence the children with whom they interact.

While motherhood is a serious responsibility and demanding work, it is also a powerful ministry. Mothers have the privilege of shaping a life, influencing a family, and making an impact on a generation. Every day God challenges a mother to diligently teach His truths to her children (see Deut. 6:6-9).

Motherhood has great rewards (see Prov. 31:28). For all Christian mothers, the greatest promise for child rearing is recorded in Proverbs 22:6:

> Train up a child in the way he should go,
> And when he is old he will not depart from it.

Whether you are a biological mother or a spiritual mother, all women of God are called to influence others for Him. As you remember the importance of created life, be a mother who is devoted, influential, tender, and nurturing. Mothers are truly blessed by God and are truly blessings to others!

THIS WEEK'S LIFE VERSES

" 'For this child I prayed, and the Lord has granted me my petition. ... Therefore I also have lent him to the Lord; as long as he lives he shall be lent to the Lord' " (1 Sam. 1:27-28).

35

THIS WEEK'S LESSONS

Day 1: Eve: God's Special Creation

Day 2: Hannah: A Devoted Mother

Day 3: Naomi: An Influential Mother-in-Law

Day 4: Mary, the Mother of Jesus: A Tender Caretaker

Day 5: Lois and Eunice: Mothers of Nurture

DAY 1

EVE

GOD'S SPECIAL CREATION

THIS WEEK'S LIFE VERSES

*" 'For this child I prayed, and the Lord has granted me my petition. ... Therefore I also have lent him to the Lord; as long as he lives he shall be lent to the Lord' "
(1 Sam. 1:27-28).*

TODAY'S LIFE LESSON
Grace

TODAY'S BACKGROUND SCRIPTURES
Genesis 2:18-25; 3–4

Eve was not only the first woman on earth but also the first wife, the first mother, and the first grandmother. When we study the life of Eve, we learn why women are God's special creation. God created Eve as Adam's companion, a helper in his God-given task. Today God continues to create women for the purposes of serving Him and ministering to others. God gives life and love to women as gifts of His abundant grace.

 Read today's background Scriptures, Genesis 2:18-25; 3–4.

THE CREATION OF GOD

Unlike the animals, Eve was a unique creation. Taking a bone from Adam's side, God created her as a woman and a wife. Both man and woman were created in God's image (see Gen. 1:26-27) with equal worth and value but with different roles and functions. In addition to being a helper to her husband, Eve was assigned by God to have children. God blessed the couple with children.

Genesis 4 begins the story of Eve's family. She gave birth to three sons, and from these sons came all future generations. Eve's name actually means "the mother of all living" (Gen. 3:20).

Motherhood did not bring only joy to Eve. Because of her sin she suffered pain in childbirth, and because of her rebellion against God her children faced the power of sin. Cain became jealous of his younger brother, Abel, and killed him. God judged Cain's sin but also protected him. This murder teaches a profound biblical truth about the sanctity of life. All life comes from God. He creates every person for a purpose. Human life is sacred, and God alone is responsible for its termination. Women today need to hear the message of the value of all human life.

 What are ways you can uphold the sanctity of human life?

_____

_____

THE WRATH OF GOD

Eve was not only the first woman and the first mother mentioned in the Bible but also the first sinner. She was both recognized as a unique creation of God and cursed as a willing pawn of Satan.

Read about the couple's temptation and fall in Genesis 3: 1-19. Focus on Eve as you answer these questions:

How did Eve's sin affect her? _____

_____

How did Eve's sin influence Adam? _____

_____

How has Eve's sin tarnished all humanity? _____

_____

37

Now think about how your sin affects others.

Eve was created pure and holy, but she chose to disobey God. When she decided to value her own desires rather than God's will, she chose to receive the consequences of sin: separation from God, separation from others, and separation from the garden of Eden.

THE GRACE OF GOD

Angry when Eve chose to sin and tempted Adam to sin also, God sent them from the garden. Though God's wrath is real, His grace is abundant. Grace is the undeserved acceptance and love received from God to provide salvation and forgiveness.[1] As often as His children choose to sin, God chooses to forgive those who repent. God took the initiative to restore His relationship with Adam and Eve, and He takes the initiative to offer forgiveness to His children who repent.

Find 1 John 1:9 and write this promise in the margin.

Be aware that when you choose to sin, you open yourself to God's wrath. But also be receptive to His grace when you are sorry for your sin and confess it to Him.

Although Eve was "the mother of all living," she was also the mother of all dying. Through her life and lineage both sin and grace entered the world. Eve suffered the consequences of her own sin and witnessed the sinfulness of her son, Cain, and his descendants. Eve was the first sinner, but she was also the first to receive God's grace.

By God's grace Eve was forgiven, and her relationships were restored. She had children, though she suffered pain in childbirth and heartache in parenting. Amid Eve's pain over the loss of Abel, she conceived another son, Seth. He lived a godly life, and through his lineage Jesus Christ was born into the world.

Eve was the first sinner, but she was also the first to receive God's grace.

Eve truly experienced the mixed blessings of motherhood. Throughout history mothers have known joys and sorrows similar to Eve's. Today women rejoice and weep over their children's choices. While Eve's life teaches the wages of sin, Eve also exemplifies God's grace to forgive and restore His children.

 Recall the times God has forgiven you. Pray, thanking Him for His amazing, abundant grace.

38

Day 2

Hannah
A Devoted Mother

Many biblical scholars agree that Hannah personifies the ideal in motherhood. What made Hannah such a respected mother? What characteristic best explains her style of motherhood? One word that accurately describes Hannah's character is *devotion*, which may be defined as *giving up oneself or one's time or energy to some purpose, activity, or person.* Hannah unselfishly put God and others first. Her devotion to God was evident through her persistent prayers and faithful obedience. Her devotion to her husband continued despite her barrenness. Her devotion to her long-awaited son persisted even as she gave him to the Lord. Hannah's life of devotion is a shining example for mothers today!

 Read today's background Scripture, 1 Samuel 1:1–2:21.

Devoted to Marriage

Hannah, whose name means *gracious*, married Elkanah, a Levite of Ramathaim Zophim, a town 5½ miles north of Jerusalem. Levites assisted the priests in many religious rites and were later integrated into the administration of the government. Like many godly men of his day, Elkanah followed the common custom of polygamy. Though children are blessings of God, God did not approve of polygamy to ensure descendants. In fact, God gave Adam one wife, taught oneness in marriage, and designed marriage to be a complementary relationship between two persons (see Gen. 2:18-22). Elkanah married Hannah, who became his favorite wife. Then he married Peninnah, who gave him many children. Hannah was obviously distraught over her inability to give her husband descendants. Her rival, Peninnah, teased Hannah about her childlessness.

Though frustrated by her inability to conceive and tormented by her jealous rival, Hannah was devoted to her marriage, and her husband was devoted to her. Elkanah was generous to Hannah, giving her a double offering when they visited the tabernacle. The Scripture says, "He loved Hannah, although the Lord had closed her womb" (1 Sam. 1:5). He tried to comfort her with words of encouragement. Later he respected Hannah's wishes in raising their son, Samuel.

Has your devotion to your husband increased or decreased since you were first married? Why?

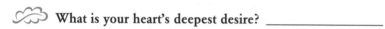

Hannah's devotion to her marriage in spite of disappointment is a witness to wives today.

DEVOTED TO GOD

During the period of the judges Israel was at one of its lowest points in history. Moral and spiritual failure followed the Israelites' disobedience to God. Materialism and ruthlessness were prevalent, but Hannah remained faithful to God. In her despair she did not turn from God. In fact, she drew closer to Him.

At one point Hannah's pain was so acute that she could not even voice her prayers: "Hannah spoke in her heart; only her lips moved, but her voice was not heard" (1 Sam. 1:13). Have you ever hurt so deeply that you couldn't find words to pray? Hannah's experience teaches us that God hears our hearts and answers our prayers.

What is your heart's deepest desire? _____

Pray about this desire regularly. The Holy Spirit will help you express your prayer even when you cannot find the words to do so.

God gave Hannah the desire of her heart—a son. In gratitude she offered a prayer of praise. Hannah's beautiful prayer reflects an intimate relationship with God developed in the midst of trials. Mary, the mother of Jesus, voiced a similar prayer of praise. Read and compare portions of these two godly mothers' prayers in the margin.

Hannah praised God for who He was and what He had done in her life. Mary praised God for His majesty and His mighty works. Women today need to express praise to God for His love, power, and grace. God deserves our devotion!

Stop and praise God. Express your devotion to Him because He is God and because you love Him.

DEVOTED TO MOTHERHOOD

Hannah was devoted to God, her husband, and her son. After many years of waiting and praying, God gave Hannah a child. Even in

**Hannah's Prayer
(1 Sam. 2:1-10)**

" 'My heart rejoices in the Lord;
My horn is exalted in the Lord' " (v. 1).
" 'The bows of the mighty men are broken,
And those who stumbled are girded with strength' " (v. 4).
" 'Those who were full have hired themselves out for bread,
And the hungry have ceased to hunger' " (v. 5).
" 'The Lord kills and makes alive;
He brings down to the grave and brings up' " (v. 6).

**Mary's Prayer
(Luke 1:46-55)**

" 'My soul magnifies the Lord
And my spirit rejoices in God my Savior' " (vv. 46-47).
" 'He has shown strength with His arm;
He has scattered the proud in the imagination of their hearts' " (v. 51).
" 'He has filled the hungry with good things;
And the rich He has sent away empty' " (v. 53).
" 'He has put down the mighty from their thrones,
And exalted the lowly' "
(v. 52).

39

naming him, Hannah gave glory to God. She named her son Samuel, saying, " 'Because I have asked for him from the Lord' " (1 Sam. 1:20). Hannah dedicated her child to God before he was born, then gave him to God after his birth.

 Read Hannah's words of commitment in 1 Samuel 1:28, in the margin. If you have a child, have you dedicated that child to the Lord? In the margin write Hannah's prayer in your own words. Then pray those words from your heart for you and your child.

When Hannah had weaned Samuel, she took him to the temple, where he remained under the tutorship of Eli, the priest. Hannah was able to see her son only once a year when she and Elkanah returned to the temple for the annual pilgrimage. Her devotion to God led to separation from her son. Hannah's heart must have ached for her much loved son.

Even today when mothers give their children to God, they don't know how God will use them or where He might take them. But like Hannah, whose son Samuel grew to be an outstanding prophet, Christian mothers today who dedicate their children to the Lord know that His plan for their lives is best. Follow Hannah's example of devotion to her husband, to God, and to her son.

" 'I also have lent him to the Lord; as long as he lives he shall be lent to the Lord' "
(1 Sam. 1:28).

40

DAY 3

ΠAOMI
AN INFLUENTIAL MOTHER-IN-LAW

Human nature is easily influenced by people or things. We are strongly swayed by others' examples. That is why God's Word encourages believers to influence others for good and not for evil (see Rom. 12:21).

Christian women have the responsibility and privilege of making a significant difference in the lives of other women. In Titus 2:3-5 Paul challenged older women to teach younger women to be godly. Christian women need to be godly role models for other women. That is the hallmark of the Christian virtue of influence, a virtue modeled by Naomi in the Book of Ruth.

Read today's background Scripture, Ruth 1–3.

AN INFLUENTIAL WIFE
Naomi was living happily in Bethlehem of Judah with her husband, Elimelech, and their two sons when a famine struck. Elimelech decided to move his family to Moab, where food was more abundant.

THIS WEEK'S LIFE VERSES
" 'For this child I prayed, and the Lord has granted me my petition. ... Therefore I also have lent him to the Lord; as long as he lives he shall be lent to the Lord' "
(1 Sam. 1:27-28).

TODAY'S LIFE LESSON
Influence

TODAY'S BACKGROUND SCRIPTURE
Ruth 1–3

If your family had to relocate, would you respond with faith or bitterness? Naomi probably regretted the move but submissively followed her husband to the distant land. Her faith in God gave her courage to face this transition and later sustained her when her husband and sons died.

When the widow Naomi decided to return to her homeland, she tried to return alone, but her daughters-in-law insisted on traveling with her. Elimelech and Naomi must have had a profound influence on the young women, who were willing to leave their own country to remain with Naomi. Although Orpah decided to stay in Moab, Ruth journeyed with her mother-in-law to Bethlehem. Both women were destitute, but they had their faith to depend on.

41

An Influential Mother-in-Law

While in Moab, Naomi's sons had married Moabite women. The Moabites were a pagan race that had resulted from the incestuous relationship between Lot and his elder daughter (see Gen. 19:36-37). Throughout history the Moabites and Israelites were enemies. Frequently, the prophets pronounced judgment on the people of Moab (see Isa. 15:1-9). Though Jewish law forbade marriage to foreigners, Naomi warmly embraced Ruth and Orpah despite their racial and religious differences. Her faith in God was a great testimony to her daughters-in-law.

How can mothers influence their daughters? And how can mothers-in-law influence the women their sons have married? As relationships are developed, the older woman's life can have a profound impact on the younger woman.

Naomi's faith in God was a great testimony to her daughters-in-law.

How did Naomi influence Ruth? Closely examine the following Scriptures and write what this committed woman did to nurture her daughter-in-law.

Ruth 1:11-13: _____

Ruth 2:19: _____

Ruth 3:2-4: _____

Naomi acted unselfishly. She showed interest in Ruth and offered wise counsel. Her godly influence made a difference in Ruth's life.

When two persons unite in friendship or in marriage, two parties are involved. A healthy relationship involves reciprocal love and affirmation. Ruth was influential in the life of her mother-in-law.

Reread the Scriptures on the following page and record what Ruth did to return love to Naomi.

Ruth 1:10: _____

Ruth 2:14-18: _____

Ruth 3:5-6: _____

Ruth expressed loyalty to her beloved mother-in-law, unselfishly responding to her and graciously accepting Naomi's wise counsel.

If you are married, how has your mother-in-law influenced you?

_____

Express appreciation for her influence and return her love.

An Influential Friend

Naomi and Ruth were relatives because Ruth married Naomi's older son, Mahlon. But the two women also became friends. They developed a close mentoring relationship and were bonded by love.

Friendship doesn't just happen. It takes work. Here are some requirements for friendship to begin and grow:

- Friends must have an attitude of acceptance. Naomi accepted Ruth though she was from a different country and race.
- Friends enjoy each other's company. It is obvious that Naomi and Ruth enjoyed being with each other. Naomi's bitterness over the loss of her husband and sons was replaced by joy as she spent time with Ruth.
- Friends must be committed to each other. Naomi reciprocated Ruth's commitment. She remained loyal to her daughter-in-law.
- Friends openly communicate with each other. Naomi talked frankly with Ruth about how to secure Boaz's affection.
- Friends share their faith with each other. Naomi obviously shared with Ruth her faith in God, because Ruth made a commitment to adopt that faith (see Ruth 1:16).

As Naomi and Ruth settled in Bethlehem, they depended on and cared for each other. Naomi counseled Ruth. Both women shared great joy when Ruth married Boaz and gave birth to Obed, whose lineage included King David and Jesus Christ. Ruth kept her pledge of devotion to Naomi that she expressed so beautifully in Ruth 1: 16-17, and Naomi's godly influence was evident in Ruth's life.

Review "An Influential Friend" above. In week 2 you were asked to identify someone you would consider mentoring. How can you use the suggestions listed to develop or deepen a friendship with that person? Write your ideas in the margin.

42

Friendship takes work.

DAY 4

MARY, THE MOTHER OF JESUS

A TENDER CARETAKER

THIS WEEK'S
LIFE VERSES
" 'For this child I prayed, and
the Lord has granted me my
petition. ... Therefore I also
have lent him to the Lord;
as long as he lives he shall be
lent to the Lord' "
(1 Sam. 1:27-28).

TODAY'S LIFE LESSON
Tenderness

TODAY'S
BACKGROUND
SCRIPTURES
Luke 1–2; John 2:1-11

Have you ever wondered why God has blessed you abundantly or why He has placed you in a position of responsibility? Mary of Nazareth must have asked these questions when the angel announced to her the coming birth of Jesus Christ. She was a humble young girl living in obscurity in the little village of Nazareth. While Mary was of the tribe of Judah and the line of David, God chose her not because of her genealogy but because of her godliness. This humble young woman would become the most honored woman of all time when she gave birth to the Messiah.

Little is known about Mary, though many people revere her. Her quiet spirit and gentle manner spoke powerfully. Throughout history artists have depicted Mary in royal clothes to reflect her beauty and character. The Scriptures, however, make clear that Mary had inner beauty: true peace and joy from God. Artists also show Mary with a radiant countenance to reflect her spirit. These representations accurately show tenderness on the face of Mary, the mother of Jesus.

 Read today's background Scriptures, Luke 1–2; John 2:1-11.

A TENDER CALL

Among all of the godly Jewish women in Palestine, why did God choose Mary of Nazareth to give birth to the Savior of the world? In His divine wisdom God chose a woman who would humbly follow His call. As a naive, innocent young maiden Mary was totally dependent on God for protection and provision.

Three of the Gospels and Acts mention Mary, but only Luke includes a full account of the announcement about Jesus' birth, an event that would change the course of history. Luke 1:26-38 describes Mary as "highly favored" and "blessed," one chosen by God for a very special task. Initially, Mary was startled when an angel appeared to her and spoke. After the explanation and with a calm faith, Mary obediently accepted God's call. Her words were tender; read Luke 1:38 in the margin. She spoke these words from her heart.

TENDER CARE

The virgin Mary gave birth to Jesus, then with Joseph, a simple carpenter, reared Jesus. Mary nurtured Him for 30 years before He began His full-time ministry. All mothers bear a great responsibility in parenting, but Mary had the additional challenge of caring for the

" 'Behold the maidservant of
the Lord! Let it be to me
according to your word' "
(Luke 1:38).

Savior of the world. The Scriptures do not reveal how Mary mothered Jesus, but we know that she showed Him great love and instilled in Him godly virtues. Mary is a worthy example for mothers today.

The Scriptures give a glimpse of Jesus as a child. According to Jewish tradition, He was circumcised when He was 8 days old. Then He was dedicated to the Lord in a temple ceremony in Jerusalem after Mary's 40 days of purification. Mary and Joseph followed the practices of the law of Moses in rearing their holy Son. They marveled as young Jesus was recognized as the Messiah first by Simeon, a devout man, and then by the prophetess Anna.

Luke 2:39-52 describes the Messiah's childhood growth. Reread this passage. How did Mary help Jesus understand how to—

be obedient to God's call? (See Luke 2:41-42.) _____

_____

thirst for knowledge? (See Luke 2:40,46-49.) _____

_____

love people? (See Luke 2:51-52.) _____

_____

Mary's tender heart must have been filled with joy as Jesus "increased in wisdom and stature, and in favor with God and men" (Luke 2:52). As Mary taught the Scriptures to Jesus, He learned about the prophecies of the Old Testament and discovered that He was the fulfillment of those prophecies. The mother who cared for Him tenderly and met His physical and personal needs was worried about Jesus when He remained at the temple to learn from the teachers. But again and again, tender Mary remembered the destiny of her Son and poured out on Him a mother's love.

Like Mary, how can you train your child to—

be obedient to God's call? _____

_____

thirst for knowledge? _____

_____

Tender Mary remembered the destiny of her Son and poured out on Him a mother's love.

44

love people? _____

_____

Tender Concern

Mary and Joseph reared Jesus in a godly home. By word and example they taught Him to be obedient to God, to thirst for knowledge, and to love other people. Mary herself had been faithful to God's call. She continued to learn about God and His will for her Son's life, and she always demonstrated love toward others.

Mary's tender concern for others is clearly seen in John 2:1-11, when Jesus performed His first public miracle. Jesus, His disciples, and His mother were among the guests at a Jewish wedding in Cana of Galilee. In New Testament times a wedding could last as long as a week, so you can imagine Mary's alarm when the hosts ran out of wine. Compassionate Mary sought assistance for the people from her all-powerful Son. Initially, Jesus rebuked His mother, but then, being directed by the Holy Spirit, He turned the water in six stone pots into wine. Mary responded tenderly to the needs of those around her. As a mother she wanted to instill in her Son a concern for others.

Mary cared unselfishly for her Son and for others. Her tender heart broke as Jesus was rejected by men, scorned, abused, and crucified at Calvary. As Mary stood beneath the rugged cross, this mother's grief must have been unbearable. But God strengthened her hurting heart, and Jesus tenderly spoke His last words of love to His mother: " 'Woman, behold your son' " (John 19:26).

Sometimes your heart breaks when your children suffer or experience pain. God can provide strength and hope as you rear them in Him. Let Mary be your example of tenderly nurturing your children to faith in Jesus Christ and of a life of humble obedience.

45

Day 5

Lois and Eunice
Mothers of Nurture

As the apostle Paul discipled young Timothy, he wrote to him: "Without ceasing I remember you in my prayers night and day, greatly desiring to see you, being mindful of your tears, that I may be filled with joy, when I call to remembrance the genuine faith that is in you, which dwelt first in your grandmother Lois and your mother Eunice" (2 Tim. 1:3-5). Lois and Eunice nurtured Timothy spiritually, preparing him for a fruitful ministry. Grandmothers and mothers today are encouraged to nurture their children in the Lord and into Christian ministry, as Lois and Eunice did.

This Week's Life Verses

" 'For this child I prayed, and the Lord has granted me my petition. ... Therefore I also have lent him to the Lord; as long as he lives he shall be lent to the Lord' " (1 Sam. 1:27-28).

TODAY'S LIFE LESSON
Nurture

TODAY'S
BACKGROUND
SCRIPTURES
Acts 16:1-3
2 Timothy 1:1-8

46

Read today's background Scriptures, Acts 16:1-3; 2 Timothy 1:1-8.

A GODLY GRANDMOTHER

Most grandmothers would agree that having grandchildren is one of life's greatest joys! Grandparenting is also a serious responsibility. Grandmothers have the privileges of influencing their children's children and of ministering to them in special ways.

The term *grandmother* is used only once in the Bible, although numerous grandmothers are mentioned by name. In 2 Timothy 1:5 Paul identified Lois as Timothy's grandmother. Lois was a devout Hebrew woman who taught the Old Testament Scriptures to her daughter and grandson. She lived in Lystra during the time of the apostle Paul's ministry. Paul recognized her genuine faith as a significant influence in Timothy's life and ministry.

How can a grandmother be a godly influence on her grandchildren? The Bible teaches about the impact adults can have on young people.

Write ways the following Scriptures can teach grandmothers how to invest their lives in the next generation.

Deuteronomy 6:7-9: _____

Psalm 121: _____

Proverbs 13:22: _____

Jeremiah 32:17: _____

Grandmothers can talk about their faith and the Bible, relating the Scripture to each child. Grandmothers can be used by God to lead their grandchildren to salvation in Jesus Christ. Grandmothers can pray with their grandchildren and for their protection and spiritual growth. A godly grandmother, like Lois, leaves a spiritual inheritance to her children's children. Grandchildren need to be reminded of the awesome power of God to face life's challenges.

A FAITHFUL MOTHER

Young Timothy was blessed. He had a godly grandmother and a godly mother who made a powerful impact on his life. His mother, Eunice, was a Jewess who married an unnamed Greek Gentile. Very little of Eunice's family background is recorded in Scripture. Her husband is not mentioned by name in the Bible and may have died when Timothy was young. The faith of Eunice and her mother, Lois, is applauded by Paul in his letter to young Timothy. Eunice nurtured her son spiritually and physically.

Read 2 Timothy 3:14-17. What did Eunice teach her son?

_____

_____

How did those teachings help Timothy?

_____

_____

How can you teach your children the things Eunice taught Timothy?

_____

_____

Timothy's faithful mother, Eunice, is a model for Christian mothers today. Mothers face the daily challenges of parenting, but they reap the abundant rewards of a loving relationship. When the prophet Isaiah sought to illustrate God's unending love for His children, he used the love of a new mother as his example:

> *"Can a woman forget her nursing child,*
> *And not have compassion on the son of her womb?*
> *Surely they may forget,*
> *Yet I will not forget you" (Isa. 49:15).*

A mother's love for her child is enduring, but God's love is even greater. As a mother demonstrates her undying love for her children, she has opportunities to teach her children about the Father's eternal love for them.

Like Timothy, I have been blessed with a strong heritage of faith. Throughout my childhood and well into my adult years, my faith was nurtured by two godly grandmothers. They prayed for me, encouraged my Christian growth, and taught me the Scriptures. My mother also nurtured my faith. She always made sure I was in church. In fact, she often tells young mothers how she reared her daughters with the help of the Lord and the church. She taught me the Scriptures and the importance of memorizing them. As a teenager I didn't always appreciate her pressure to memorize Scriptures, but those Scriptures still fill my heart and guide my life. I am grateful for a mother and two grandmothers who nurtured my faith and for a mother who continues to pray for me faithfully.

As a mother demonstrates her undying love for her children, she has opportunities to teach her children about the Father's eternal love for them.

An Obedient Child

With a mother and a grandmother who were committed to the Lord and diligent in their spiritual instruction, it is no surprise that Timothy became a godly man and a faithful disciple of Christ. However, not all faithful mothers and grandmothers have godly children. Some children rebel against their family's faith. Children in rebellion break not only their mothers' hearts but also God's heart.

The Bible tells the stories of some rebellious children. One of the best-known accounts is of the prodigal son in Luke 15:11-32.

Read this parable, paying particular attention to verses 20-24. How did the father's faith influence his rebellious son?

_____

Because of his upbringing the son recognized that he had sinned and deserved to be disowned. The father had faith that his son would return home. When he did, the father's faith was the source of the compassion and love with which he embraced and forgave his son.

Ruth Bell Graham, the wife of evangelist Billy Graham, has often shared the story of their once rebellious son Franklin. During his wildest teenage years Ruth, a worried mother, wrote in her journal: "Every time I pray especially for him God says: Love him. ... Which seems odd because I love every bone of him. But God means show it. Let him in on the fact. Enjoy him. You think he's the greatest let him know you think so."[2] That is good advice for mothers who face the challenge of rearing children.

What promise does God give to mothers and grandmothers who try to nurture their children in the faith?

> _Train up a child in the way he should go,_
> _And when he is old he will not depart from it (Prov. 22:6)._

Write Proverbs 22:6 in your own words as a prayer for your children.

_____

_____

Thank God for the privilege of nurturing your children to faith in Him.

Thank God for the privilege of nurturing your children to faith in Him.

[1]Adapted from Trent C. Butler, ed., _Holman Bible Dictionary_ (Nashville: Holman Bible Publishers, 1991), 573.
[2]Patricia Cornwell, _Ruth, A Portrait_ (New York: Doubleday, 1997), 186.

WEEK 4
WORKING WOMEN IN THE BIBLE

OVERVIEW OF WEEK 4

This week you will—
- examine the integrity of Huldah the prophetess;
- observe the diligence of the Proverbs 31 woman;
- experience the joy of young Rhoda;
- learn about priorities from Lydia;
- see a picture of competence in Priscilla.

WOMEN IN THE WORKPLACE

According to the Bureau of Labor and Statistics, 44 percent of the work force in 1996 were women.[1] Therefore, we can assume that many Christian women are in the workplace today. While all Christian women encounter life's many demands, those in careers face unique challenges. The responsibilities of a personal life and a professional life are at times overwhelming. In addition, Christian working women must be positive witnesses of God's love to their coworkers.

Mary Whelchel returned to the workplace as a young divorced mother who needed to support her child. When she realized that churches rarely offer programs that meet the specific needs of working women, she founded a radio ministry called "The Christian Working Woman," which blended biblical teaching and practical advice for Christian women in the work world. When asked about the spiritual impact of working outside the home, Mary Whelchel responded: "The workplace is a battlefield where you either die or grow. But for those who latch on to the Lord, it's an environment where you'll be challenged to grow in your faith in exciting ways."[2]

Christian working women who depend on God for wisdom and strength can be conscientious workers and effective witnesses. The lives of godly businesswomen testify of God's grace. Faithful Christian workers must be diligent, honest, loyal, respectful, and hard-working. Many working women in the Bible provide examples for career women today. If you are one of the many Christian women in the workplace, this week you will learn ways to remain faithful as you work and witness. If you do not work outside the home, God can use these biblical examples to teach you the virtues of integrity, discipline, joy, proper priorities, and competence.

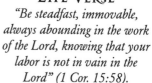

THIS WEEK'S LIFE VERSE

"Be steadfast, immovable, always abounding in the work of the Lord, knowing that your labor is not in vain in the Lord" (1 Cor. 15:58).

49

THIS WEEK'S LESSONS

Day 1: Huldah: A Prophetess of Integrity

Day 2: The Proverbs 31 Woman: A Disciplined Woman

Day 3: Rhoda: A Joyful Maid

Day 4: Lydia: A Businesswoman with Proper Priorities

Day 5: Priscilla: A Competent Worker

DAY I

HULDAH
A PROPHETESS OF INTEGRITY

50

TODAY'S LIFE LESSON
Integrity

**TODAY'S
BACKGROUND
SCRIPTURE**
2 Kings 22:14-20

Ⅰn Bible times God called prophets to proclaim specific messages. God spoke through the prophets to predict the future, to clarify God's will, to foretell historical events, and to write His Word for His people. Prophets influenced almost every institution in Israel, including the temple and the government. Huldah was an Old Testament prophetess whose life of integrity spoke as loudly as her words of prophecy.

 **Read today's background Scripture, 2 Kings 22:14-20.**

A PROPHETESS OF INTEGRITY

During the Babylonian Exile in the first century B.C. the Israelites enjoyed the blessings of obedience to God but did not consistently obey Him. God raised up prophets who warned the Israelites that God's judgment was inevitable if they did not consistently obey Him. Among them was Huldah, who lived in Jerusalem when it was ruled by King Josiah, following the reigns of the great kings of Israel, David and Solomon. Josiah became the king at the young age of eight and reigned for 31 years. Baal worship prevailed, and riotous living was rampant. When Hilkiah the priest found the Book of the Law and shared it with King Josiah, the king was disturbed by its words of judgment and sought the counsel of the prophetess Huldah.

Huldah was married to Shallum, the son of the keeper of the royal wardrobe. She was probably an official member of the royal court. It is certain that her wise counsel was frequently sought by King Josiah, the priest, and the Hebrew leaders. Though Jeremiah and Zephaniah were well-known prophets during this time, the king consulted Huldah. God had appointed her as a significant prophetess.

Reread 2 Kings 22:15-20 to learn God's message that Huldah communicated to King Josiah. Summarize what she said.

_____

_____

Huldah not only confirmed the authenticity of the Book of the Law, but she also prophesied judgment on the people who had forsaken God and a peaceful death for Josiah the king. What was the result of Huldah's prophetic message? King Josiah had the courage to follow God and lead his people back to God and righteous living.

Four times Huldah said, "Thus says the Lord" or "says the Lord" (see 2 Kings 22:15-16,18-19). She acknowledged the message from God and the need for repentance. Huldah was a prophetess of integrity used by God. Her words from God were a catalyst for change in the people's behavior.

Read Deuteronomy 13:1-5; 18:18-22. List characteristics of a prophet of integrity.

_____

_____

Huldah had the spiritual gift of prophecy, which is the reception and declaration of a word from God. Huldah used her gift in proportion to her faith (see Rom. 12:6) for Christian service, not for personal edification (see Eph. 4:12). She did not share her own dreams and visions but proclaimed the truth from God. History proves that her prophecy was correct. She did not accept praise or credit for her prophecies that were fulfilled. Huldah loved the Lord and walked in His ways. She did not have to fear the consequences of false prophecy. Instead, she spoke with integrity God's word to the people.

Huldah was a faithful prophetess who used her spiritual gift with integrity as she served the Lord. Her personal conviction and steadfast commitment to truth are testimonies to Christian working women today.

Huldah spoke with integrity God's word to the people.

Name ways you can express in your job your commitment to God's truth.

_____

_____

A Life of Integrity

Integrity refers to singleness of heart or mind, the development of blameless character and exemplary behavior. The Old Testament uses the term *integrity* often to describe an attitude of the heart and a godly walk (see Gen. 20:5-6; 1 Kings 9:4; Prov. 19:1; 20:7). In other references the Old Testament describes a person of integrity (see Ps. 7:8; 25:21; 26:1; 101:2). In the New Testament *integrity* is mentioned once in Titus 2:7, in which Christians are encouraged to be a godly example, "in doctrine showing integrity." Repeatedly in the New Testament singleness of heart or mind is discussed (see Matt. 5:8; 6:22; Jas. 1:7-8; 4:8).

Are you a person of integrity? How would your friends describe your character?

_____

_____

If any shortcomings in this area come to mind, stop and pray about them, asking the Lord to help you be a person of integrity.

Huldah, the prophetess, had integrity. She had singleness of heart and lived a righteous life. Her prophecy was effective because her character did not tarnish her witness.

In your workplace demonstrate your singleness of heart in your words and deeds. Be an example of Christ to those who work around you. Have integrity and honesty in your business dealings, and God will use you and reward you in a mighty way. Read Proverbs 20:7 in the margin. A Christian who walks and works with integrity is blessed by God. A life of integrity is a blessing to all!

Though included in only one account in Scripture, Huldah had an important job. No matter how large or small an assignment appears to be, in God's plan all work for Him is important. Huldah was a messenger of God, a voice for communicating God's word of truth. She fulfilled her divine task with integrity.

Huldah's personal integrity allowed her to be an effective prophetess of God. God can use Christian women today as witnesses of Him in the workplace if they live lives of integrity. Commit yourself to be, like Huldah, a worker with integrity.

52

"The righteous man walks in his integrity;
His children are blessed after him" (Prov. 20:7).

DAY 2

✝ THE PROVERBS 31 WOMAN

A DISCIPLINED WOMAN

Few women in Scripture have been admired as much as the Proverbs 31 woman. She was trustworthy, organized, and loving. She worked diligently in her home and community. Her strength obviously came from God. What a role model for busy Christian women today!

THIS WEEK'S
LIFE VERSE
"Be steadfast, immovable,
always abounding in the work
of the Lord, knowing that your
labor is not in vain in the
Lord" (1 Cor. 15:58).

 Read today's background Scripture, Proverbs 31:10-31.

Through the Proverbs 31 woman God provides insight into being a woman of faith. Enjoy the following paraphrase of Proverbs 31:10-31.

A Proverb for Supermom

If you can find a truly good wife, she is worth more than
all the diamonds in Tiffany's!
She holds the flashlight and doesn't make fun
while her husband repairs the drippy faucet for the seventh time.
She sews on Girl Scout patches while
watching "Sesame Street" with her four-year-old;

And treats her teen-age son's basketball team to pizza
after they lose the big game.
She gets up before dawn to go jogging
after setting out the box of granola and fresh fruit for her family.
She earns a real estate license and puts a down payment
on a duplex with her commission.
She keeps her floors shiny with Mop-n-Sop,

And clips coupons.
She pays the monthly bills while watching the 11 o'clock news.
She repairs her kids' tennies with Zippy Glue and
cleans out her closets for the homeless.
She enjoys knitting sweaters while watching football with her own
#1 hero.
When she gets all dressed up, her king of the castle
thinks she looks like a queen.
When she and her husband attend the White House Prayer
Breakfast,
she doesn't faint when the president shakes her hand.
She works out at Believercize
and softens her wrinkles with Vitamin E Oil.
She smiles and says "Good Morning" to the cranky next-door
neighbor.
She keeps score for her younger son's Little League games
and agrees to teach Sunday School one more year.
She goes to PTA meetings and choir practice, even when
it means missing the conclusion to a mini-series she is following.
Her husband tells her, "Honey, you're the greatest,"
and her children rise up and call her ... collect.[3]

Glenda Palmer

A Diligent Woman

The Proverbs woman was diligent. Though Scripture does not specify that this woman worked outside the home, few would question her diligent work ethic. She was hard-working and industrious. Some have suggested that she may have had a cottage industry, weaving fabric

53

and making clothes in her home for sale in the marketplace. Several verses in Proverbs 31:10-31 describe the way the Proverbs 31 woman worked. She worked willingly (v. 13), early in the morning (v. 15), creatively (v. 19), unselfishly (v. 20), and hard (v. 27).

 In the previous sentence underline the characteristics that apply to you as a Christian working woman.

The diligence of the Proverbs 31 woman inspires Christian women to be hard-working and conscientious.

A DETERMINED WOMAN

The Proverbs 31 woman was determined. She worked from morning to night. She worked diligently and never gave up. She persevered in every task. Perseverance is an important virtue of Christian working women. It means *faithful endurance and patient steadfastness even in the face of opposition, attack, and discouragement.*[4] Perseverance not only sees a task through but also produces patience (see Jas. 1:2-4 in the margin). In all her work the Proverbs woman was determined.

Whether or not she was employed outside the home, her many skills could have provided gainful employment. The Proverbs 31 woman possessed the skills of a weaver (v. 13), merchant (v. 14), realtor (v. 16), farmer (v. 16), designer (v. 18), and seamstress (v. 22). No matter what her position, the Proverbs woman was determined. She did everything wholeheartedly, and she always did her best.

How determined have you been in your work recently? Mark your status on each continuum.

Continued tirelessly	Gave up in frustration

Completed each task	Let other responsibilities distract me

Unwavering in my resolve	Easily disillusioned

If you found that your determination has wavered, resolve to work diligently. Look to the Lord as your source of strength.

A DISCIPLINED WOMAN

The Proverbs 31 woman was also disciplined. To get all her work done, she had to be a good manager. She developed skills to manage her time, her resources, and her spiritual gifts. If Christian working

"Count it all joy when you fall into various trials, knowing that the testing of your faith produces patience. But let patience have its perfect work, that you may be perfect and complete, lacking nothing" (Jas. 1:2-4).

women can use their time, resources, and gifts wisely, they will be very productive. Certain skills are necessary for efficient work. Management skills don't come easily, but developing those skills through discipline is quite beneficial.

The Hebrew word for *wisdom* means *a skill for living.*[5] The Proverbs 31 woman had a skill for living. She developed the skills for her work through discipline. In addition to personal discipline she also received help from God. Divine discipline helped her get her work done. "Divine discipline is Spirit-controlled discipline of oneself."[6] It is not innate but learned from God. Christian women need divine discipline.

 How can you develop divine discipline?

55

Personal discipline and spiritual discipline are necessary for busy working women, who have many responsibilities. Discipline is not easy. In fact, it can be difficult and painful. However, God promises great rewards for Christian women who practice discipline in His power. Read Hebrews 12:11 in the margin.

The Proverbs 31 woman may seem like a superwoman, but every Christian woman can and should develop her primary attributes of diligence, determination, and discipline.

"No discipline seems pleasant at the time, but painful. Later on, however, it produces a harvest of righteousness and peace for those who have been trained by it" (Heb. 12:11, NIV).

DAY 3

RHODA
A Joyful Maid

Many contemporary songs speak of the joy we have in the Lord. That was the song of Rhoda, the young maid of John Mark's mother. And that should be the song of Christian working women today.

Joy is the happy state that results from knowing and serving God. The word *joy* is found more than 150 times in the Bible,[7] and many other words are also used to describe it. Obviously, joy is an important Christian virtue. It is a fruit of the Holy Spirit (see Gal. 5:22-23) and should be evident regardless of the circumstances (see Jas. 1:2-3). Biblical joy is clearly different from earthly happiness. Joy is eternal, while happiness is temporal. God wants all of His children to be filled with joy. Joy is to be a blessing to the believer and a witness to others.

The joy of the Lord in your life can be a great attraction to unbelievers in your workplace. Often those without the Lord are looking for happiness and meaning in life. When they see a joy-filled Christian, they have hope, and they want the same joy in their lives.

THIS WEEK'S LIFE VERSE
"Be steadfast, immovable, always abounding in the work of the Lord, knowing that your labor is not in vain in the Lord" (1 Cor. 15:58).

TODAY'S LIFE LESSON
Joy

TODAY'S BACKGROUND SCRIPTURE
Acts 12:12-17

Rhoda teaches Christian women today to be joyful in their work.

If you are joyful in your work as Rhoda was, you can draw your coworkers to Christ.

☁ Read today's background Scripture, Acts 12:12-17.

JOYOUS SERVICE

Though of foreign origin, Rhoda was given a Greek name meaning *rose*. She lived in Jerusalem in about A.D. 43 and was the maid of John Mark's mother, Mary. As a maid she worked long hours and had no life of her own. Scripture records no family history or personal background since she was a servant. Her mistress, Mary, was apparently a wealthy widow who opened her home for church members to pray. On this occasion Rhoda probably served not only her mistress but also the church members.

Many servants were not happy in their work, but Rhoda seemed to enjoy herself. She worked late into the night while the church people prayed for Peter's release from prison. Her work did not seem to be a burden but a blessing. Rhoda teaches Christian women today to be joyful in their work.

☁ Are you joyful on the job? Why or why not?

A JOYOUS MESSAGE

During this time of religious persecution Christians feared for the life of Peter, who had been imprisoned by Herod, and they constantly prayed for him. The prayer meeting at the house of Mary, John Mark's mother, was interrupted by a knock on the door. Imagine Rhoda's joy when, after they had prayed for hours for Peter's release from prison, she heard his voice outside the door. In her excitement Rhoda forgot to open the door for Peter before running to tell the people about his release.

☁ Has God ever answered a prayer for you that was immediate and visible? Describe the way you felt.

As Rhoda told the Christians about Peter, she must have been so excited that she seemed crazy. At first the people didn't believe her. Then they tried to convince her that she had seen an angel, but Rhoda was confident of her encounter and thankful for answered prayer. The young girl's sorrow had quickly been replaced by joy when she saw that Peter was free.

Rhoda was not the only person in Scripture whose state of mind was questioned. She was in good company. Jesus was called crazy by His relatives: " 'He is out of His mind' " (Mark 3:21). Festus pronounced Paul out of his mind because of the gospel he preached (see Acts 26:24). But like these, Rhoda was not crazy. She had a love for her work and an excitement about God's work.

Rhoda was a special messenger to the early church. Her words reaffirmed the Christians' faith. Certainly it is important to be clear and composed when relating a message, but enthusiasm about the message is always appreciated. Joy should always be apparent when sharing the gospel. Rhoda was joyful about her good news!

A Joyous Response

Though initially the church members thought Rhoda was crazy, they opened the door when Peter continued knocking. They were astonished to see the beloved disciple who had been imprisoned, and their astonishment immediately turned to joy. After Peter described his release, everyone went out to joyously relate Peter's story.

Christians can share their joy with other Christians as God works in their lives. A believer's natural response to God's work should be great joy.

Do you feel joy when you do God's work? If not, why not? What adjustments do you need to make to serve the Lord with joy?

For 15 years I was the director of speech pathology in a large medical center. My workplace was my mission field. Many times my greatest witnesses were my positive attitude and joyful spirit. One Monday an unsaved colleague laughingly told me about an experience she had had with her children on Saturday. While running errands, they stopped at a car wash sponsored by the youth at a neighborhood church. The excited youth were raising money for a summer mission trip. Her young children commented that "all these people sound happy like Mrs. Rhonda." My friend wanted to know if all Christians are happy. We should be.

Little else is known about Rhoda, but the young girl's enthusiasm has made a profound impression on Christians through the centuries. The young maid who was joyful in her service shared her joy with the other believers. Joy is often contagious. In the workplace it is important for Christian women to be filled with joy despite circumstances. Joy can be a testimony of God's grace and a witness of His love. Be a joyful worker like Rhoda.

Joy can be a testimony of God's grace and a witness of His love.

Would others say that you have the joy of the Lord? If not, ask God to give you this fruit of the Spirit. Constantly surrender your thoughts to Him so that you do not allow circumstances to destroy your joy.

DAY 4
LYDIA
A Businesswoman with Proper Priorities

58

Today's Life Lesson
Proper priorities

Today's Background Scripture
Acts 16:12-15,40

" 'Give your entire attention to what God is doing right now, and don't get worked up about what may or may not happen tomorrow' " (Matt. 6:33, The Message).

"Yes, all the things I once thought were so important are gone from my life. Compared to the high privilege of knowing Christ Jesus as my Master, firsthand, everything I once thought I had going for me is insignificant" (Phil. 3:8, The Message).

Working women face no greater challenge than juggling life's many demands. While work often occupies the most time in a day, it is important to keep priorities in proper perspective. Work is important, but other things matter to God and others. Keeping Christ at the center of your life is a challenge no matter what other responsibilities claim your time.

Lydia was a businesswoman in Philippi who successfully balanced the many priorities in her life. While she worked full-time as a merchant, she also had a significant ministry. Lydia entertained believers in her home, ministered to Paul and Silas, and housed the first European church. This industrious businesswoman had her priorities straight. When we have proper priorities, God can use us mightily.

Read today's background Scripture, Acts 16:12-15,40.

GOD
Lydia responded to Paul's message at the river. Immediately after her conversion she began serving the Lord. The Lord became the first priority in her life.

Read Matthew 6:33 and Philippians 3:8 in the margin and underline a Christian's primary priority.

What holds top priority in your life? _____

Lydia's newly found faith was so strong that she led her whole household to faith in Jesus Christ or made sure that they heard Paul's message. When God is first in your life, witnessing is a natural result.

What kind of witness are you in your workplace? Write the names of colleagues you can witness to as you pray for them.

_____

Recommit yourself to maintaining proper priorities. Like Lydia, put God first.

FAMILY
The Bible clearly says that Christians are to seek God first. The next priority should be your family. You have a responsibility to yourself and your loved ones. Work should not consume all of your time.

Read the Scriptures in the margin to recall why your family should be of great importance.

Since Scripture doesn't mention a husband and Lydia worked outside the home, she is often thought to have been single. Her household was her family. She immediately shared her faith with her household or asked Paul to do so, and they were baptized. Lydia put Christ and the members of her household before her work.

For a married Christian woman, your husband is a precious priority. Christian mothers must consider their children a primary focus. If a Christian woman does not care for her family, why should an employer expect her best? A job is no reason to neglect your family.

Let Lydia be your example of a Christian businesswoman who put God and others before her work.

WORK

What Lydia did for a living was mentioned in the Scriptures only briefly: "She was a seller of purple" (Acts 16:14). Her relationship with God and her concern for her household were most noteworthy. Christian women today should have the same priorities: God first, others next, and work last. Too often, the demands of the job keep work at the forefront.

Still, the Scriptures teach that work is important. Workers are to fulfill their responsibilities of employment (see 1 Thess. 4:11-12) and to work for the Lord (see Col. 3:17). Paul often wrote about diligence in work and Christian behavior.

Read Romans 12:11 in the margin. Do you think Paul was remembering Lydia as a diligent worker who served unselfishly? Write a statement describing how you work.

_____

_____

While Lydia put God and others before her job, she was not lazy in her work. Instead, her fervent spirit made her an effective worker as well as a faithful witness. She faithfully served the Lord without neglecting her other responsibilities.

When I "retired" from my work in speech pathology, I thought I would have more time for God. But new priorities quickly claimed my time, and again I struggled to keep Christ as the central focus of my life. Like Lydia, I had to set priorities to keep the Lord first.

Lydia kept Christ at the center of her life while balancing her other priorities. Let her remind you to maintain proper priorities and to keep Christ at the center of your life.

"A man shall leave his father and mother and be joined to his wife, and they shall become one flesh" (Gen. 2:24).

*"Children are a heritage from the Lord,
The fruit of the womb is a reward" (Ps. 127:3).*

"Wives, submit to your own husbands, as to the Lord. Husbands, love your wives, just as Christ also loved the church and gave Himself for her" (Eph. 5:22,25).

59

"Not slothful in business; fervent in spirit; serving the Lord" (Rom. 12:11, KJV).

How are you managing your priorities? Number the areas below 1, 2, and 3 according to their present positions in your life.

_____ God   _____ Family   _____ Work

Pray, asking God to help you set or maintain proper priorities. Commit to keeping God the central focus of your life. All of your other priorities should flow from your relationship with Him.

60

DAY 5
PRISCILLA
A COMPETENT WORKER

Competence is "being qualified, capable, able or adequate to do a job."[8] Priscilla was a competent worker in New Testament times. A capable worker, she always tried to do more. Competence in the workplace can be a positive witness. Christian working women are challenged to do their best and to keep learning.

Read today's background Scriptures, Acts 18:1-3,18,26; Romans 16:3-4; 1 Corinthians 16:19; 2 Timothy 4:19. Note in the following verses what you learn about Priscilla's character or work.

Acts 18:2: _____

Acts 18:18: _____

Acts 18:26: _____

Romans 16:3: _____

1 Corinthians 16:19: _____

2 Timothy 4:19: _____

A COMPETENT TENTMAKER

Priscilla (or Prisca) was a Jew of Asia Minor. Little is known about her family background. Her name is always mentioned with her husband's name, Aquila. Obviously, they had a close relationship and were partners in ministry. After their conversion they worked to spread the gospel.[9]

Priscilla and her husband were in business together as tentmakers. Priscilla must have been very competent to be in business with her husband in a male-dominated world. Paul, also a tentmaker, met

THIS WEEK'S LIFE VERSE
"Be steadfast, immovable, always abounding in the work of the Lord, knowing that your labor is not in vain in the Lord" (1 Cor. 15:58).

TODAY'S LIFE LESSON
Competence

TODAY'S BACKGROUND SCRIPTURES
Acts 18:1-3,18,26
Romans 16:3-4
1 Corinthians 16:19
2 Timothy 4:19

Priscilla and Aquila and worked with them. They must have helped one another professionally and personally. Priscilla was no doubt respected among the Christians of her day. Her competence as a tentmaker and her ministry as a Christian made a positive impact for Christ.

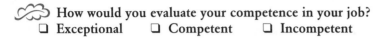 **How would you evaluate your competence in your job?**
❏ **Exceptional**   ❏ **Competent**   ❏ **Incompetent**

What can you do to increase your competence at work?

61

_____

A Competent Christian

Although we know little about Priscilla's ability as a tentmaker, we know more about her commitment as a Christian. The Scriptures indicate that Priscilla had a growing relationship with Jesus Christ. Even though she was a busy working woman, she apparently made time to study the Scriptures. She shared with others what she learned.

Priscilla and Aquila had the opportunity to teach Apollos, an Alexandrian Jew who became an influential minister and a powerful preacher. These committed Christians shared biblical doctrine with this gifted young man. They poured their spiritual insights into one who had a platform for the gospel.

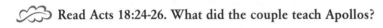 **Read Acts 18:24-26. What did the couple teach Apollos?**

_____

_____

Apollos understood baptism as a sign of repentance, but he did not associate it with new life in Christ through Jesus' death and resurrection. Priscilla and Aquila enabled Apollos to exalt Jesus Christ through a proper understanding of Christian baptism. As a maturing believer you may have the opportunity to teach others who will be used by God. But first you must be found faithful. Like Priscilla, you must be a competent Christian who knows God's Word.

Paul was grateful to meet this godly Christian couple who joined him in ministry. Acts 18:2 says, "[Paul] found a certain Jew named Aquila … with his wife Priscilla." Paul met many believers during his ministry, but Priscilla and her husband were memorable. Their deep faith and vibrant ministry got Paul's attention. Competence in your work and commitment to your Lord can get the attention of the persons you work for and with. Be a faithful witness!

Competence in your work and commitment to your Lord can get the attention of the persons you work for and with.

62

Priscilla and Aquila
persevered in sharing the
gospel message.

How can you be a competent Christian on the job?

A COMPETENT CHURCH LEADER

Priscilla and her husband, Aquila, were apparently influential among the "churches of the Gentiles" (Rom. 16:3). Born in Pontus, Aquila probably met and married Priscilla in Rome. The Roman emperor Claudius banished all Jews from Rome in A.D. 49, so Priscilla and Aquila moved to Corinth.[10] There they met Paul. The exact time of their conversion is uncertain, but they served the Lord with Paul in Corinth. Later they journeyed with Paul to Ephesus to spread the gospel.

This committed Christian couple made a powerful impact on several early churches. Read 1 Corinthians 1:10-17 and Ephesians 1:15-21 to learn the challenges the couple faced.

Priscilla and Aquila encountered dissension, false teaching, and persecution, but they persevered in sharing the gospel message. They were competent Christian leaders who led by the authority of God and the testimony of the Holy Spirit.

Are you fully competent in your ministry for the Lord? What can you do to develop your competence?

Paul had great admiration for Priscilla. First, he admired her competence as a tentmaker. Then he recognized her commitment as a Christian. And finally, he praised her faithfulness in ministry. Paul thanked her for risking her life for him and for giving her all for the church (see Rom. 16:3-4). Your competence in your work, life, and ministry will also be appreciated by those you work with.

[1]Jo-Ann L. Yu, "The Employment Situation: November 1997," Bureau of Labor Statistics, <http://www.bls.gov/ftp://146.142.4.23/pub/news.release/History/empsit.120597.news> (05 December 1997).
[2]Judith Briles, Luci Swindoll, and Mary Whelchel, *The Workplace: Questions Women Ask* (Portland: Christianity Today, Inc. in conjunction with Multnomah, 1992), 7.
[3]Glenda Palmer, "A Proverb for Supermom," *HomeLife*, May 1995, 45. Used by permission.
[4]Dorothy Kelley Patterson and Rhonda Harrington Kelley, eds., *The Woman's Study Bible* (Nashville: Thomas Nelson Publishers, 1995), 2123.
[5]Alice Mathews, *A Woman God Can Use* (Grand Rapids: Discovery House Publishers, 1990), 158.
[6]Rhonda Kelley, *Divine Discipline* (Gretna, LA: Pelican Publishing Company, 1992), 38.
[7]Trent Butler, ed., *Holman Bible Dictionary* (Nashville: Holman Bible Publishers, 1991), 819.
[8]David B. Guralnik, ed., *Webster's New World Dictionary of the American Language*, 2nd college ed. (New York: The World Publishing Company, 1970), 289.
[9]Herbert Lockyer, *All the Women of the Bible* (Grand Rapids: Zondervan Publishing House, n.d.), 122.
[10]Patterson and Kelley, *The Woman's Study Bible*, 1842.

WEEK 5
WOMEN LEADERS IN THE BIBLE

OVERVIEW OF WEEK 5
This week you will—
- understand what leadership is from Miriam;
- aspire to be just and fair like Deborah;
- seek to be courageous like Esther;
- consider the dignity of Anna;
- learn to serve humbly like Phoebe and Damaris.

WOMEN IN LEADERSHIP
When God created heaven and earth, He recognized the need for order. He created man and woman in His image and gave them different roles in the world. Because of human nature God determined our need for leadership and established lines of authority. Human beings need someone to follow—a leader. Men were designed to be the leaders of the home. Women were given the leadership responsibilities of loving their husbands, nurturing their children, mentoring other women, and serving the Lord.

God endows many women with the spiritual gift of leadership. Women need certain traits to be effective leaders. Susan Hunt and Peggy Hutcheson have identified four qualities essential to leadership: vision, passion, commitment, and risk taking.[1] It is essential for leaders to dream dreams and set goals. Leaders need to be enthusiastic and passionate about their work. Positive energy is contagious. Commitment to the task is a necessary ingredient for leadership. Every job must be seen through to the end. A leader must also be a risk taker. Faith doesn't always know the end result, so risks must be taken. These are just a few important qualities of leadership.

Several women in the Bible held positions of leadership, and women today can learn from their examples. In this week's study you will examine the lives of these women to learn about godly leadership. If you are not presently a leader, you can still develop qualities of leadership like justice, courage, dignity, and humility. God may want to develop your leadership skills and call you into service. Remember, God never calls you to do anything He doesn't equip you to do.

If you are in a position of leadership, let these biblical women set the pace for you. God has always anointed women to lead others to the saving grace of Jesus and to a meaningful life in the Spirit.

63

THIS WEEK'S LESSONS
Day 1: Miriam: A Natural Leader

Day 2: Deborah: A Just Judge

Day 3: Esther: A Courageous Queen

Day 4: Anna: A Dignified Prophetess

Day 5: Phoebe and Damaris: Humble Laborers

DAY I
Miriam
A Natural Leader

**THIS WEEK'S
LIFE VERSE**
*" 'Who knows whether you
have come to the kingdom
for such a time as this?' "
(Esth. 4:14).*

TODAY'S LIFE LESSON
Leadership

**TODAY'S
BACKGROUND
SCRIPTURES**
Exodus 2:4-10; 15:20-21
Numbers 12:1-15; 20:1
Micah 6:4

Miriam, Moses' older sister, was a natural-born leader. From her earliest appearance in Scripture when she was baby-sitting Moses beside the Nile River, Miriam had natural leadership abilities. She took charge when her brother was found in the bulrushes. Later, she became a leader of the people of Israel.

How would you define *leadership*?

_____

_____

Leadership is a gift from God that is not accomplished or acquired. It is the ability to influence people toward a common goal. Miriam was born with God-given abilities as a leader. Her positive family background prepared her for leadership. Her life experiences shaped her leadership skills. Her brothers, Aaron and Moses, were role models of leadership. It is no wonder that Miriam became an outstanding leader.

Read today's background Scriptures, Exodus 2:4-10; 15:20-21; Numbers 12:1-15; 20:1; Micah 6:4.

NATURAL LEADERSHIP
Miriam was the daughter of Jochebed and Amram and the sister of Aaron and Moses. Jochebed must have recognized Miriam's natural leadership abilities, because at an early age she gave Miriam serious responsibilities.

Reread the first account of Miriam in Exodus 2:4-10. What do you discover about Miriam's character?

_____

_____

It was a dangerous time in Egypt. Pharaoh had decreed that all Hebrew boys would die. Jochebed wanted to save her son, Moses. Knowing that Miriam was trustworthy, her mother sent her to the river to watch Moses in a basket. Miriam was intelligent. When Pharaoh's daughter found Moses, Miriam offered to find a wet nurse for the baby and then enlisted her mother. Miriam was courageous; she was not afraid of a powerful princess. Miriam was also loving; she obviously cared deeply for her mother and brother.

🗨 **Do you have natural leadership abilities like Miriam? Look over the characteristics of leadership listed in the margin.[2] Check the characteristics you feel that you possess.**

God needs women with natural leadership abilities to develop their skills and to use them for His glory as Miriam did.

FALTERING LEADERSHIP

The next account of Miriam is found in Exodus 15:20-21, which identifies her as a prophetess. Miriam led the Israelite women in singing a song of victory. Jubilantly she sang:

> *"Sing to the Lord,*
> *For He has triumphed gloriously!*
> *The horse and its rider*
> *He has thrown into the sea!" (v. 21).*

Miriam gratefully sang about her faith. Later, Miriam's song turned sour. She began to rebel against Moses' leadership. Numbers 12:1-15 records that although she condemned the ancestry of Moses' wife, it was his authority she really criticized. God became angry about Miriam's faltering leadership. She was no longer faithful, godly, and loving but bitter, critical, and judgmental. God punished Miriam for her treatment of Moses.

🗨 **What happened to Miriam? (See Num. 12:9-10.)**

_____

_____

Miriam remained leprous for seven days, and then God restored her. Many Christian women have faltered in their leadership. Miriam's suffering should warn leaders to remain faithful to God.

🗨 **Have you experienced failure as a leader because you acted in the flesh instead of following God's direction? Explain.**

_____

_____

_____

When we fail, we can seek God's restoration and thank Him for His forgiveness.

❏ enthusiasm
❏ flexibility
❏ innovation
❏ availability
❏ ability to listen
❏ dependability
❏ accountability
❏ ability to nurture/disciple
❏ encouragement
❏ delegation
❏ ability to train
❏ transparency
❏ ability to evaluate

65

*"I brought you up from the land of Egypt,
I redeemed you from the house of slavery;
And I sent before you Moses, Aaron, and Miriam" (Mic. 6:4).*

Strong Leadership

Miriam is not mentioned by name in the Scriptures from the time of her rebellion until her death. Certainly her self-will was broken during her seven leprous days outside the camp. We can hope that she lived the rest of her life humbly, submissive to God's leadership.

Miriam died in Kadesh in the Wilderness of Zin after roaming with the Israelites for 40 years. Like Moses and Aaron, Miriam did not reach the Promised Land. She must have been disappointed and discouraged at the time of her death. The woman with natural leadership abilities had faltered in her faith. She fell short of her goal and died just before the Israelites entered the Promised Land.

Yet in spite of her failure Miriam was remembered by the Israelites. Read Micah 6:4 in the margin. What a profound legacy of leadership! The Lord's words indicate that Miriam was still a leader in His eyes.

What have you learned about Miriam's leadership that you can apply to your leadership responsibilities now or in the future?

_____

_____

Miriam was a natural-born leader who stumbled and fell. But because of God's forgiveness, her leadership was restored, and her influence continued. Let Miriam remind you that the quality of your leadership is determined by your reliance on God and by your willingness to let Him lead through you.

Day 2

Deborah
A Just Judge

This Week's Life Verse
" 'Who knows whether you have come to the kingdom for such a time as this?' "
(Esth. 4:14).

Today's Life Lesson
Justice

Life is not fair! Many would agree with that statement because life brings trials and suffering. Often people are not treated fairly. That is true today, and it was true in Old Testament times. After Joshua led the Israelites into the Promised Land and before kings reigned, God raised up judges to lead the people of Israel fairly. Under God's direction these judges, who were both political and spiritual leaders, led the Israelites in fighting their oppressors.

Among all the judges of that time, only one female judge is mentioned. Deborah was a just judge who righteously led her people. Read in the chart in the margin on page 67 the judges who led Israel between 1375 and 1050 B.C. Deborah was one of many great leaders.

Although Deborah's responsibility as a judge was to help the people of Israel withstand their oppressors, the Canaanites, she did much more. She influenced her people to return to God and created a positive impression of leadership. Deborah was truly one of the greatest women leaders in the Bible.

 Read today's background Scripture, Judges 4–5.

THE BACKGROUND OF A JUDGE

The name *Deborah* means *bee* in Hebrew. The judge and prophetess Deborah must have lived the symbolism of a busy bee. In addition, " 'science confirms the ancient belief that, of all the animal kingdom, the bee ranks among the highest in intelligence.' ... 'So Deborah stands out as among the wisest of all the Old Testament women.' " This "bee" certainly had a fatal sting on her enemies, the Canaanites.[3]

Little is known about Deborah's background. No personal genealogy is given, but her marital status is documented. Judges 4:4 reveals that Deborah's husband was Lapidoth, whose name means *torches*. Although nothing is specifically said about Lapidoth, Deborah's success as a leader suggests that he must have been comfortable with his wife's fame and recognition and was therefore probably supportive and affirming.

On the other hand, Scripture records much about the life of Deborah. She was respected as a person and a leader. Judges 5, an ancient Hebrew poem, recognizes Deborah as a mother in Israel. There is no evidence that Deborah had children of her own, but through her righteous leadership she became a mother to her people, their source of spiritual nurture.

THE JUSTICE OF A JUDGE

Deborah's reign can be divided into three parts:

1. Judges 4:4-10. Deborah, as prophetess and judge, sat under a palm tree, where the children of Israel came to her for judgment. She received a word from the Lord and called Barak to convey her God-given battle strategy to defeat the Canaanites. At his request Deborah accompanied the military commander and his 10,000 men into battle. Her plan from God led to victory for the Israelites, who defeated the enemy commander Sisera and the Canaanites.
2. Judges 4:12-16. Deborah led the Israelites in one of their greatest victories. In a battle as dramatic as the crossing of the Red Sea the Canaanites, riding in chariots, fell under Barak's sword. Only Sisera himself was left alive.
3. Judges 4:23-24. After Barak led the Israelites to conquer the Canaanites, Deborah continued to lead her people. King Jabin of Canaan was subdued, and Israel grew stronger.

Most scholars believe that Deborah composed the victory song she

TODAY'S
BACKGROUND
SCRIPTURE
Judges 4–5

67

Judges
- Othniel (Josh. 15:16-19; Judg. 1:11-15; 3:7-11; 1 Chron. 4:13)
- Ehud (Judg. 3:12-30; 4:1)
- Shamgar (Judg. 3:31; 5:6)
- Deborah (Judg. 4–5)
- Gideon (Judg. 6:1-8,32; Heb. 11:32)
- Abimelech (Judg. 8:33– 9:57; 2 Sam. 11:21)
- Tola (Judg. 10:1-2)
- Jair (Judg. 10:3-5)
- Jephthah (Judg. 10:6– 12:7; Heb. 11:32)
- Ibzan (Judg. 12:8-10)
- Elon (Judg. 12:11-12)
- Abdon (Judg. 12:13-15)
- Samson (Judg. 13:1– 16:31; Heb. 11:32)

sang with Barak.[4] Recorded in Judges 5, the song describes the call of the people, God's past deliverance, oppression in Israel, God's righteous acts, Deborah's call, Israel's response, the battle, Jael's triumph, and the anxiety of Sisera's mother. In God's divine plan justice was complete. Under Deborah's leadership the people of Israel overcame their enemies and celebrated victory. With the people's hearts now turned back to God, Deborah's reign as judge ended with rest: "The land had rest for forty years" (Judg. 5:31).

Do you deal justly with others? Examine your relationships. Do you deal justly with—

your spouse?	❏ Yes ❏ No
your children?	❏ Yes ❏ No
your coworkers?	❏ Yes ❏ No
your friends?	❏ Yes ❏ No
your coworkers in ministry?	❏ Yes ❏ No
those you lead?	❏ Yes ❏ No
strangers?	❏ Yes ❏ No

God is your source of justice in dealing with others. Ask Him to help you relate justly to others as you lead.

THE JUDGMENT OF A JUDGE

As a prophetess Deborah was a spiritual leader for her people. As a judge she was their military leader. Her leadership influenced them nationally and personally. Her messages from God provided direction for religious thought, and her strategies for defense provided protection from military overthrow. As a prophetess and a judge she issued pronouncements that were always just; they were from God. Deborah brought to the people God's message that He would lead them in victory over the Canaanites. She played an important role in leading the people back to God.

Deborah, God's prophetess and judge, left a legacy of justice as she solved the people's problems, made wise decisions, courageously accompanied the troops in battle, motivated others to action, and inspired the people to follow God. Christian women today are challenged to leave a legacy of just leadership that always follows God's direction.

Deborah played an important role in leading the people back to God.

DAY 3

ESTHER
A COURAGEOUS QUEEN

A powerful drama unfolds in the Old Testament Book of Esther. The setting is ancient Persia during the first century B.C. The events of Esther took place during the reign of King Ahasuerus (also known by the Greek name Xerxes).

 Read today's background Scriptures, Esther 2; 4; 7; 9.

Let's identify the five major characters in this historical epic. King Ahasuerus, who is introduced in the first two verses of the Book of Esther, reigned in Persia from 486–465 B.C. A powerful king, he ruled from the capitol city of Shushan (or Susa). Ahasuerus was in the early years of his monarchy when the story of Esther begins.

Queen Vashti appears only in chapter 1 of Esther. By birth Vashti was a Persian princess. Her name means *beautiful woman,* indicating that she must have been one of the loveliest women in Persia. Vashti refused the request of King Ahasuerus to appear before the men of the kingdom at the end of a national feast. Consequently, she was dethroned. Nothing is known about the exiled queen after that.

Haman was a wealthy, influential officer in the court of King Ahasuerus. He was an Agagite, a nomadic people who hated the Jews. When Ahasuerus promoted him to a high position, tension began as he conspired against the Jews.

Mordecai was a godly Jew living in exile in Persia. He was introduced as "the son of Jair, the son of Shimei, the son of Kish, a Benjamite" (Esth. 2:5). His ancestry, strongly Jewish, included Saul, the first king of Israel (see 1 Sam. 9:1-2). As Esther's only living relative Mordecai cared for her like his own daughter.

Esther (or Hadassah), whose name means *a star,* was an orphaned Jewish girl living in Persia when she was chosen by Ahasuerus to be his queen. The story of this rising star is a testimony of courage to Christian women today. She was a godly leader with courageous faith.

COURAGE AND CHARACTER

Esther was apparently a natural beauty whose appearance was pleasing to King Ahasuerus. When he began searching for a new queen, Ahasuerus had many young women brought to him, including Esther. Each focused for one year on her appearance before going to the king. Esther was different. When her turn came, "she requested nothing but what Hegai the king's eunuch, the custodian of the women, advised" (Esth. 2:15). Smitten by Esther's beauty, Ahasuerus chose her. The poor, orphaned Jewish girl became a queen!

THIS WEEK'S
LIFE VERSE
" 'Who knows whether you
have come to the kingdom
for such a time as this?' "
(Esth. 4:14).

69

TODAY'S LIFE LESSON
Courage

TODAY'S
BACKGROUND
SCRIPTURES
Esther 2; 4; 7; 9

Review the following verses and write the characteristics of Esther that are revealed.

Esther 2:9: _____

Esther 2:10: _____

Esther 2:12-15: _____

Esther 2:16-17: _____

Esther apparently had grace and charm, which were immediately visible to the king. Her outer beauty was matched by her inner beauty. She was obviously restrained and wise, knowing the right moment to reveal her Jewish identity to the king. Esther was teachable; she learned from her uncle, Mordecai. She was unselfish, modest, and genuine. She found favor with everyone around her, not just the king. Humble, Esther respected authority. She possessed many qualities that are important for Christian women in leadership today.

Courage and Compassion

Esther had reigned only briefly when her uncle, Mordecai, learned of a plot against the king's life. Mordecai told Esther, who informed King Ahasuerus of the evil plan. The guilty men were executed, and the king's life was spared. However, life for the Jews soon became difficult.

Haman, an influential officer in the king's court, was promoted to the second highest position in the land. Haman hated the Jews. Because Mordecai did not honor him, Haman convinced King Ahasuerus to issue a decree that all people must bow or be executed. This decree meant certain death for Esther, Mordecai, and all Jews since they would bow only to God. At this point King Ahasuerus did not know that Esther was a Jew. When Esther learned of Haman's plot against the Jews, she was "deeply distressed" (Esth. 4:4).

Read Esther 4:14 in the margin. Mordecai believed that God would use Esther to save her people. God had placed Esther in a significant position of leadership for a very specific reason.

" 'Who knows whether you have come to the kingdom for such a time as this?' " (Esth. 4:14).

Has God ever put you in a certain place at a certain time for His divine purpose? Explain.

_____

Esther and her people fasted and prayed for God to direct Esther. Then she planned a banquet for the king and Haman. During the banquet Esther courageously revealed to the king Haman's evil plot against Mordecai and the Jews. She revealed herself as a Jew and identified Haman as wicked. In anger King Ahasuerus condemned Haman to death by hanging on the same gallows Haman had prepared for Mordecai. God had used Esther to save her people. Because of her compassion Esther had the courage to defend them.

Courage and Conquest

Esther's courage had far-reaching results for her people. In the final chapters of Esther the Jews overpowered their enemies and resumed their position of authority.

Esther led her people in a celebration to thank God for their deliverance. The Feast of Purim, which continues to be celebrated by Jews today, celebrates the deliverance of the Jews from Haman's evil plot.

Esther's appearance in Jewish history was no coincidence. She played a significant role in saving her people. Her godly leadership continues to be celebrated by present-day Jews. God raised up this courageous queen to fill an important role at a crucial time in history. God continues to raise up godly Christian women to fill important roles today. Be a courageous leader like Esther!

71

Check ways you can be courageous in a leadership role you presently hold.
- ❑ Standing up for truth
- ❑ Being willing to try new areas of ministry
- ❑ Confronting with compassion
- ❑ Boldly asking for God's direction
- ❑ Being a mentor or a role model
- ❑ Maintaining upright character

Pray for courage to develop as a leader in these areas.

Day 4

Anna
A Dignified Prophetess

Dignity is "the quality or state of being worthy, honored, or esteemed."[5] People who live godly lives are worthy of esteem and honor. The Proverbs woman wore dignity as her clothing (see Prov. 31:25, NASB). Her strength and godliness were visible to all who knew her. Though dignity begins within, it quickly overflows into actions, attitudes, and speech.

Paul instructed women to adorn themselves with good works (see 1 Tim. 2:9-10). In other words, wear godliness, which results in dignity. In Colossians 3:12-14 Paul challenges us to put on virtues

This Week's Life Verse
" 'Who knows whether you have come to the kingdom for such a time as this?' " (Esth. 4:14).

Today's Life Lesson
Dignity

such as mercy, kindness, humility, meekness, longsuffering, forgiveness, and love. Practicing these virtues develops dignity. Dignity is the crown of a godly life.

The prophetess Anna possessed dignity because of her godly character and her service as a prophetess. Christian women who lead today can also be recognized for their dignity.

 Read today's background Scripture, Luke 2:36-38.

72

A PERSON OF DIGNITY

The prophetess Anna's name means *grace*. A secular dictionary and a Bible dictionary define *grace* differently. According to *Webster's, grace* is "beauty or charm ... an attractive quality, goodwill."[6] *Holman Bible Dictionary* defines *grace* as "undeserved acceptance and love received from another, especially the characteristic attitude of God."[7] While Anna may have possessed beauty and charm, her grace was from God. Her dignity resulted from her commitment to God.

 Review Luke 2:36-38 and complete the biographical information about Anna.

Anna was a _____

She was the daughter of _____

She was of the tribe of _____

She lived with her husband _____

She was now a _____

She was _____ years old.

Like most Hebrew women, Anna married at a young age but was widowed after only seven years of marriage. As a single woman she was "married" to her ministry. Apparently a member of the resident staff at the temple in Jerusalem, for many years Anna prophesied the coming of the Messiah. Anna's days were filled with worship, prayer, and fasting.

The Scriptures introduce Anna soon after Jesus' birth. Eight days after Jesus was born, He was circumcised according to Jewish tradition (see Luke 2:21). Then He was presented in the temple after Mary's period of purification (see Luke 2:22-38). According to Jewish law, 40 days must pass after giving birth before a woman is pure before God.

Simeon was a devout Jew worshiping in the temple when Jesus was brought there by His parents. Simeon had claimed God's promise that he would not die before the Messiah appeared. The Holy Spirit revealed to him that Jesus was the Messiah. His public announcement confirmed for Mary and Joseph their Son's divine destiny.

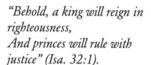 **Anna was in the temple and heard Simeon's announcement. How did Anna respond to her glimpse of Jesus?**

_____

_____

Anna instantly gave thanks to the Lord for His gift of salvation and told others about the arrival of the Messiah. We are told that Anna "did not depart from the temple, but served God with fastings and prayers night and day" (Luke 2:37). Anna was a person of dignity and honor because of her godly character. She enjoyed a close relationship with God, and she longed and prayed for Him to bring redemption to the world. Having looked forward to Christ's coming for a long time, she was obviously very excited when she saw Him.

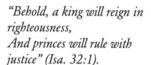 **Name someone you know who loves God and walks closely with Him. Record evidence that this is a person of dignity.**

_____

_____

A PROPHETESS OF DIGNITY

It is clear from her reaction in Luke 2:38 that Anna had previously proclaimed the divine message that Jesus Christ, the Messiah, would soon come. This gentle, elderly woman had claimed the promises of the Old Testament prophets. Prophecies like the ones in the margin foretold that the Messiah would come from the lineage of Jesse, the father of King David. He would be a righteous King, reigning in peace, and would be born in Bethlehem.

Anna's faith was rewarded when she saw the Messiah with her own eyes. Anna responded to the appearance of Jesus in a dignified way. When she saw Him, she worshiped Him. She immediately gave thanks to God for giving His Son. She hailed Jesus as the Christ and proclaimed the redemption He would bring. All believers should worship and speak of Jesus, the Savior of the world!

Anna was a dignified leader among her people. She gained their respect with her godly life. She earned their honor with her accurate prophecy of the Messiah's birth. As a result, she was crowned with dignity. Christian women who are in positions of leadership today must live godly lives of dignity.

73

"There shall come forth a Rod from the stem of Jesse, And a Branch shall grow out of his roots" (Isa. 11:1).

"Behold, a king will reign in righteousness, And princes will rule with justice" (Isa. 32:1).

"Out of Zion the law shall go forth, And the word of the Lord from Jerusalem. He shall judge between many peoples, And rebuke strong nations afar off; They shall beat their swords into plowshares, And their spears into pruning hooks; Nation shall not lift up sword against nation, Neither shall they learn war anymore" (Mic. 4:2-3).

" 'You, Bethlehem Ephrathah, Though you are little among the thousands of Judah, Yet out of you shall come forth to Me The One to be Ruler in Israel, Whose goings forth are from of old, From everlasting' " (Mic. 5:2).

⌒♥ Anna's dignity grew from her relationship with God. How can you lead with more dignity as you follow Anna's example?

_____

_____

74

THIS WEEK'S
LIFE VERSE
" 'Who knows whether you
have come to the kingdom
for such a time as this?' "
(Esth. 4:14).

TODAY'S LIFE LESSON
Humility

TODAY'S
BACKGROUND
SCRIPTURES
Romans 16:1-2
Acts 17:22-34

DAY 5
PHOEBE AND DAMARIS
HUMBLE LABORERS

The New Testament records the names of numerous women who ministered with Jesus and the disciples. The first woman to minister with Jesus was His mother, Mary, who nurtured Him in childhood (see Luke 2). Susanna supported Jesus' ministry with her energies and resources (see Luke 8:1-3). Mary and Martha of Bethany served Jesus (see Luke 10:39). And Mary Magdalene ministered to Jesus until and after His death on the cross (see John 19:25; 20:16). Women were significant colaborers with Jesus Christ.

Paul praised many women who were leaders in the early church:
- Phoebe helped many (see Rom. 16:1-2).
- Priscilla risked her life for Paul's life (see Rom. 16:3-4).
- Mary of Rome labored much for the gospel (see Rom. 16:6).
- Lydia opened her home to Paul and other believers (see Acts 16:11-15).
- Tryphena and Tryphosa labored in the Lord (see Rom. 16:12).
- Persis labored much for the Lord (see Rom. 16:12).
- Rufus's mother served as a surrogate mother to Paul (see Rom. 16:13).
- Euodia and Syntyche labored with Paul in the gospel (see Phil. 4:2-3).
- Apphia hosted the church in her home (see Philem. 2).

Women have historically filled positions of leadership in the church. God has called women to serve others, and He has equipped them to serve. Women in leadership today should model Jesus' leadership: humble service to others. Humility is a personal quality that shows dependence on God and respect for other persons. Jesus Christ's life provides the best example of humility (see Matt. 11:29; 1 Cor. 4:21; Phil. 2:1-11). Paul often discussed humility. In 2 Timothy 2:24-25 he stressed the importance of teaching with patience and humility. The New Testament teaches that Christian leaders should be humble as they serve.

The Greek world abhorred humility, associating it with weakness. Biblical humility is not weakness but meekness—strength under control. Humble Christians are not overly concerned with their own prestige (see Matt. 18:4; 23:12; Rom. 12:16; 2 Cor. 11:7). Although the world today does not appreciate meekness or humility, Christian women must seek to lead like Jesus, who served with humility.

PHOEBE: A HUMBLE SERVANT

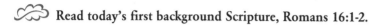 **Read today's first background Scripture, Romans 16:1-2.**

Phoebe was a Gentile Christian from Cenchrea, the eastern port city of Corinth. Paul wrote commending her to the church at Rome. Though not much is known about this New Testament woman, Paul obviously had great respect for her. Apparently, she humbly served the Lord, seeking no recognition for herself. It was Paul who praised her.

Name women in your church who lead without seeking recognition.

_____

Thank God for their humble service. Can you honestly say that you lead humbly, or do you seek recognition for your work?

_____

In prayer commit to serve the Lord with humility. Ask Him to help you do so.

Paul spoke highly of Phoebe. He called her sister because they were both God's children. He called her servant because of her tireless work for the Kingdom. He called her saint because of her godly lifestyle. And he called her helper because of her ministry to many others in addition to Paul.[8]

Review the previous paragraph as you answer: Can other believers call you—

sister? Why or why not? _____

servant? Why or why not? _____

saint? Why or why not? _____

helper? Why or why not? _____

Some Bible translations call Phoebe a deacon or a deaconess. The

Christian women must seek to lead like Jesus, who served with humility.

75

76

second phrase of Romans 16:1 in the Greek calls Phoebe *diakonos*. The Greek root means *one who ministers or serves*.[9] Therefore, Paul seems to commend Phoebe's action of service, not her position of leadership. Many women in the church today are servants who minister.

Damaris: A Humble Believer

 **Read today's second background Scripture, Acts 17:22-34.**

As Paul witnessed in the marketplace in Athens, a group of philosophers began to argue with him. They led him to Mars Hill, a hill overlooking the city of Athens, where the philosophers of the day often gathered to discuss their ideas. Referring to the city's altar to an unknown god, Paul preached a sermon that powerfully presented the gospel of Jesus Christ.

Reactions to Paul's sermon were mixed. Many mocked and sneered, but others wanted to know more. Several became believers, including Damaris. This woman was apparently well known in her hometown of Athens and probably worshiped idols before her conversion. She humbled herself to Christ's claim on her life even though she was surrounded by skeptics who mocked the gospel.

> Damaris humbled herself to Christ's claim on her life even though she was surrounded by skeptics who mocked the gospel.

In receiving Christ, Damaris acknowledged that she did not have the power to save herself. Do you regularly acknowledge that without God you would be ineffective and powerless in your everyday life and in your leadership role or ministry? Acknowledge these thoughts in prayer, at the same time praising God's goodness, power, and sovereignty.

Damaris humbled herself before God in salvation and probably went on to become a humble leader in the early church. Like Phoebe and Damaris, Christian women in leadership today must be humble and totally dependent on God as they live and serve.

[1]Susan Hunt and Peggy Hutcheson, *Leadership for Women in the Church* (Grand Rapids: Zondervan Publishing House, 1991), 38–39.

[2]Chris Adams, comp., *Women Reaching Women* (Nashville: LifeWay Press, 1997), 61.

[3]Herbert Lockyer, *All the Women of the Bible* (Grand Rapids: Zondervan Publishing House, n.d.), 40.

[4]Adapted from Dorothy Kelley Patterson and Rhonda Harrington Kelley, eds., *The Woman's Study Bible* (Nashville: Thomas Nelson Publishers, 1995), 391.

[5]*Webster's Ninth New Collegiate Dictionary* (Springfield, MA: Merriam-Webster Inc., Publishers, 1991), 354.

[6]David B. Guralnik, *Webster's New World Dictionary of the American Language,* 2nd college ed. (New York: The World Publishing Company, 1970), 605.

[7]Trent Butler, ed., *Holman Bible Dictionary* (Nashville: Holman Bible Publishers, 1991), 573.

[8]Patterson and Kelley, eds., *The Woman's Study Bible,* 1891.

[9]Ibid.

WEEK 6
WOUNDED WOMEN IN THE BIBLE

OVERVIEW OF WEEK 6

This week you will–
- learn about the security God provided for Hagar;
- understand forgiveness through the eyes of Dinah and Tamar;
- learn how to express gratitude like Mary Magdalene;
- examine the strong faith of the hemorrhaging woman;
- witness the freedom Jesus offered the woman at the well.

SUFFERING SAINTS

Society often asks, Why do bad things happen to good people? It is hard to understand why God allows suffering even among believers. God's Word teaches that suffering is inevitable (see Jas. 1:2). Yet it is temporary in the framework of eternity (see 1 Pet. 1:6). The Book of James teaches Christians how to manage suffering. Trials test a believer's faith, and they can produce endurance. Believers can take joy in their suffering because God can supply wisdom and strength.

Jesus Christ is our perfect model for suffering. Even though He was God and without sin, Christ suffered for us. First Peter 2:21-25 shows us how Jesus Christ responded to suffering. When He was unjustly treated, He did not retaliate but trusted God to judge those who wronged Him. In fact, Jesus Christ suffered for those who offended Him most. His response to suffering is our pattern for suffering.

Many women in the Bible suffered. Often, they were innocent victims of violence or mistreatment. Sometimes their circumstances brought them great suffering. When these women called out to God for help, He healed them, strengthened them, and provided for them. Wounded women today can also depend on God's comfort in their suffering.

Have you been hurt by those you love or by difficult circumstances? God wants to heal you. He wants to soothe your pain and restore your broken heart. He is the Great Physician and the Comforter. As you study this week, let the wounded women of the Bible give you hope, strength, and assurance.

If you have not been wounded personally, you know wounded women. God can use you to strengthen them. Let God teach you to depend on Him for security, forgiveness, strength, and freedom. Be grateful for a God who tenderly cares for His hurting children.

THIS WEEK'S LIFE VERSE

"As the sufferings of Christ abound in us, so our consolation also abounds through Christ" (2 Cor. 1:5).

77

THIS WEEK'S LESSONS

Day 1: Hagar: A Secure Slave

Day 2: Dinah and Tamar: Innocent Victims

Day 3: Mary Magdalene: A Grateful Disciple

Day 4: The Hemorrhaging Woman: A Strong Believer

Day 5: The Woman at the Well: From Bondage to Freedom

DAY I

HAGAR
A SECURE SLAVE

78

THIS WEEK'S LIFE VERSE
"As the sufferings of Christ abound in us, so our consolation also abounds through Christ" (2 Cor. 1:5).

TODAY'S LIFE LESSON
Security

TODAY'S BACKGROUND SCRIPTURES
Genesis 16; 21:9-21
Galatians 4:21-31

" *'Whoever listens to me will dwell safely,*
And will be secure, without fear of evil' " (Prov. 1:33).

afety and security are basic human needs. A person needs to feel protected and cared for. When safety is at risk and security breaks down, an individual feels alone, helpless, and abandoned. The Bible depicts the lives of women who felt unsafe and insecure. But God protected them and provided for them.

Read today's background Scriptures, Genesis 16; 21:9-21; Galatians 4:21-31.

Hagar was the young Egyptian maidservant of Sarah and Abraham. As a servant she had no personal rights and privileges.[1] However, she received provision and protection from her owners. Security is "freedom from fear, anxiety, danger, doubt; state of ... certainty ... or tranquility."[2] When Hagar ran away, she obviously had no security. She was alone, afraid, anxious, worried, and doubtful. Pregnant with Abraham's child, Hagar could depend only on God for help for herself and her son. God in His mercy saved their lives.

Those who are wise seek security from God. When a believer calls out to God and listens, she finds safety in Him. Read Proverbs 1:33 in the margin. God never lost sight of Hagar. He loved her, protected her, and secured her future. God offers that same security to wounded women today.

SAFE

Born into slavery in Egypt, Hagar was bought by Abraham or was given to him by Pharaoh to be Sarah's personal servant. Most Egyptians worshiped idols, but Hagar soon followed the God of her owners. Though she had little freedom, she had great freedom in the Lord. She faithfully served her masters and was provided for generously. As a slave she was expected to obey Sarah's every command.

When Sarah found herself sterile and without the son God had promised, she took matters into her own hands and gave Hagar to Abraham as a concubine to conceive his child. "Hagar's surrogate maternity was perfectly legal, though a clear violation of God's law (see Gen. 2:24) and evidence of a lack of faith on the part of Abram and Sarai."[3]

Hagar conceived a child by Abraham. Review Genesis 16: 4-6. How did Hagar feel toward Sarah?

How do you think Sarah felt toward Hagar?

_____

Although Sarah devised the plan for Hagar to bear Abraham's child, she became bitter. She was apparently jealous of Hagar's fertility and angry with the resulting circumstances. Hagar apparently had a change of heart, too. The pregnant Hagar apparently became insolent toward her childless mistress. Pride filled Hagar's heart, and her actions irritated Sarah. Sarah then complained to Abraham, unfairly blaming him for the problem. He firmly refused to accept responsibility and placed the matter back in Sarah's hands. In anger Sarah dealt harshly with Hagar. Wounded by Sarah's harsh words and treatment, Hagar left the safety and security of her home.

79

ALONE

When Hagar fled toward her home country of Egypt, she must have felt hurt, hopeless, and abandoned. However, God, her Provider, never left her. In her loneliness God reached out to her. While Hagar rested beside a spring of water in the wilderness outside Shur on the southern border of Canaan, an angel of the Lord appeared to her. The angel who appeared is thought by many to be a theophany, or an appearance of God Himself.[4] The angel of the Lord told Hagar to return to Abraham and Sarah, promising that her descendants would be numerous and giving her information about her son. Hagar obeyed the Lord and returned to Abraham and Sarah. She put aside her pride and accepted the security God provided. Her son was born and was named Ishmael, meaning "God hears." Hagar and Ishmael lived with Abraham and Sarah for about 14 years.

SECURE

After Sarah had given birth to her promised son, Isaac, tension between the women and between their sons grew, so Abraham reluctantly sent Hagar and Ishmael from his home. Hagar again found herself abandoned in the wilderness of Beersheba with her teenage son and only a few provisions. Becoming desperate when the water supply was almost depleted, Hagar placed her dying son under a shrub and cried out to God. He was still The God-Who-Sees, and again He met her physical and spiritual needs. When she opened her eyes, Hagar saw a well filled with water. God continued to be with her as He had promised, and He secured the fate of Hagar and her son.

God met Hagar's physical and spiritual needs.

 When you have been hurt, how did God minister to you?

_____

Hagar and Ishmael's miraculous deliverance is a testimony of a believer's security. God always provides for His own if His children cry out for help. Hagar's story has a happy ending. She and Ishmael dwelled in the Wilderness of Paran, and God promised that He would make of Ishmael a great nation. World history has been influenced by Hagar's son, Ishmael, who became the founder of the Arab nations.

Is a situation in your life causing feelings of insecurity? Stop and pray to The-God-Who-Sees about your need for His security. Express your total dependence on Him.

A final mention of Hagar is made in Galatians 4:21-31. Paul compared the freewoman Sarah and the bondwoman Hagar to distinguish between law and grace.[5] Hagar, the mother of Ishmael, is the old covenant (the law) given on Mount Sinai. Sarah, the mother of Isaac, is the new covenant (grace) given in Christ Jesus. Hagar, a bondwoman, gave birth to her son according to the flesh. Sarah, a freewoman, gave birth to her son according to the Spirit. Hagar was under the law, justified by works, enslaved to legalism. Sarah was under grace, justified by faith alone, free in Christ.[6]

How does the fact that you live in God's grace provide hope in your times of need?

_____

_____

Hagar's story is a powerful life lesson. In her great hurt and need she found security and provision in Him. God's grace is abundant, and in Him all wounded children can find safety, security, and hope.

DAY 2

DINAH AND TAMAR
Innocent Victims

In our world today innocent people often become the victims of crime and violence. Recently, a precious four-year-old boy was killed and several family members were injured when their car was struck by a drunk driver with multiple driving offenses. Several years ago a friend was brutally raped in her church parking lot. The Lord's heart is broken when human sin results in pain for innocent victims. But God cares for His wounded children. My friend said, "I didn't pray for that testimony, but God has used me to minister to other women who have been raped." God can redeem even the most tragic situation.

Redemption describes God's saving activity toward humankind. In the Old Testament three different Hebrew words express redemption. The first word, *padah,* refers only to the redemption of persons or other living beings. While intended for legal and commercial uses, it was later adopted for religious practices (see Ex. 21:29-30; Num. 18:15-17). The second word, *ga'al,* indicates "a redemption price in family members involving the responsibility of a next-to-kin." Boaz was Ruth's kinsman-redeemer who provided for his widowed relative (see Ruth 3:9-12). The third word, *kipper,* is used "in strictly religious concepts and practices" indicating atonement for or covering of sin.[7]

The New Testament focuses on the redemption brought by Jesus Christ. God sent His Son into the world to redeem humanity. The Redeemer gives forgiveness and eternal life to all who accept Him by faith. He continues to redeem or restore His wounded children. Jesus exchanges the evil in the world for His good.

DINAH'S BROTHERS TAKE REVENGE

Read one of today's background Scriptures, Genesis 34.

Dinah was the only daughter among the 12 sons of Jacob. Her mother was Leah, who also bore six sons. Probably, little celebration occurred at Dinah's birth since she was a girl (see Gen. 30:21). The Scriptures do not explain Dinah's name as they do for male children.

Jacob and his family had traveled to the city of Shechem in Canaan (see Gen. 33:18), where Jacob bought some land and erected a temple. One day Dinah wandered off alone to visit "daughters of the land" (Gen. 34:1). Then tragedy struck.

Dinah was violated by Shechem, the son of Hamor the Hivite, the prince of the country. Dinah was violently raped. Her father and then her brothers learned that she had been defiled.

This innocent young girl must have felt shame and guilt even though she was not at fault. Shame and feelings of disgrace often consume an innocent victim of rape. She may feel guilty for mistakes that were not hers. Healing begins when the one who was violated trusts the Lord for strength and comfort.

If you were counseling someone who had been raped, what would you want to say about the help God can provide?

_____

_____

TODAY'S LIFE LESSON
Forgiveness

TODAY'S BACKGROUND SCRIPTURES
Genesis 34
2 Samuel 13:1-32

81

God can help a woman forgive her attacker and reach out in love to others. He can protect her from feelings of anger, bitterness, and disgust. God can renew her relationship with Him and can use her as a witness of His love. God can redeem the most painful tragedy.

Dinah's story has a tragic ending. Shechem wanted to marry Dinah, but her brothers wanted revenge. At first they seemed willing to forgive. They demanded that Shechem, his father Hamor, and all of the other Gentile men of the land be circumcised according to Jewish tradition. They agreed, and every male was circumcised. However, Dinah's brothers Simeon and Levi took revenge anyway, killing all of the men and plundering the land. The rape of innocent Dinah led to destruction and death. Simeon and Levi's revenge caused their father, Jacob, to curse them from his deathbed (see Gen. 49:5-7).

God can redeem the most painful tragedy.

82

TAMAR'S BROTHER TAKES REVENGE

Read today's other background Scripture, 2 Samuel 13:1-32.

The Old Testament mentions three different women by the name of Tamar. Tamar, the daughter of David and Maacah, is the focus of this study. Tamar had one full brother, Absalom, and a half-brother, Amnon, whose father was David and whose mother was Ahinoam. Amnon fell in love with his beautiful half-sister. His cousin, Jonadab, devised a plan for Amnon to trap her. Pretending to be sick, Amnon begged David to send Tamar to nurse him. So David sent Tamar to prepare food for Amnon.

Review 2 Samuel 13:12-13. How did Tamar respond to Amnon's advances?

_____

Tamar attempted to distract Amnon, suggesting that he ask David if they could marry. But Amnon, filled with lust, "forced her and lay with her" (2 Sam. 13:14). Immediately afterward, Amnon hated her and sent her away because of the evil he had done. Tamar's pain and shame were so great that she tore her beautiful robes and put ashes on her head in grief and humiliation. Tamar's brother Absalom initially overlooked Amnon's evil act but later had him killed.

Have you ever taken revenge on someone? Did revenge help your healing process or increase your bitterness? Explain.

_____

_____

GOD FORGIVES

Both Dinah and Tamar were innocent victims of terrible injustice. Their assailants certainly didn't deserve forgiveness, but they could have sought forgiveness from God. Forgiveness comes from God and restores broken fellowship with Him. God's forgiveness is complete, everlasting, and available to all. He forgives us in salvation and continues to forgive us when we sin.

We also need to forgive others rather than to seek vengeance. Vengeance belongs to God (see Deut. 32:35). Jesus instructs us to respond with love and forgiveness (see Matt. 5:43-48; 18:21-35). Part of the healing process for wounded women today is to forgive the ones who hurt them. Christians are to acknowledge their hurt, freely forgive the offense, and confess any bitterness (see Eph. 4:31-32; Col. 3:12-15).

We don't know anything about Dinah's and Tamar's lives after these incidents, but we can hope that they sought refuge in God. Wounded women today can depend on God's comfort to heal their hurts and on God's power to help them forgive their offenders.

83

Have you been unable to forgive someone? Forgive that person now with the forgiveness that comes from God. Offer a prayer in which you forgive the person with God's help.

DAY 3

MARY MAGDALENE
A GRATEFUL DISCIPLE

Christians should be filled with gratitude. Gratitude is "a feeling of thankful appreciation for ... benefits received."[8] A Bible dictionary states that gratitude is "directed towards God, generally in response to God's concrete acts in history."[9] Heartfelt appreciation for God's many blessings should be the natural response of all believers. We should express gratitude for God's past, present, and future blessings. We should thank God for life itself.

Mary Magdalene, who ministered with Jesus, witnessed His crucifixion, and discovered the empty tomb, had an attitude of gratitude. She was a grateful disciple of Jesus.

Read today's background Scriptures, Mark 15:40-41,47; 16:1-19; Luke 8:1-2; 24:10; John 19:25; 20:1-18.

GRATEFUL IN MINISTRY

Though Mary Magdalene's name is mentioned 14 times in the Gospels, little is known about her before she met Jesus. We do not

THIS WEEK'S LIFE VERSE
"As the sufferings of Christ abound in us, so our consolation also abounds through Christ" (2 Cor. 1:5).

TODAY'S LIFE LESSON
Gratitude

TODAY'S BACKGROUND SCRIPTURES
Mark 15:40-41,47; 16:1-19
Luke 8:1-2; 24:10
John 19:25; 20:1-18

know her family background or marital status, but the Bible records that she was born in Magdala, a city on the western shore of the Sea of Galilee. It was a prosperous fishing town on a main highway to Tiberias. Mary Magdalene may have been a single businesswoman, since she had the freedom and the finances to travel with Jesus.[10]

Luke wrote that the young woman had been filled with seven demons. Her demons may have been physical, mental, or spiritual illness. Whatever her particular affliction, Mary Magdalene was healed by Jesus (see Mark 16:9).

Mary Magdalene was grateful to God for her salvation and her healing. How did she express her gratitude in Luke 8:1-3?

_____

From deep personal gratitude Mary Magdalene gave all of her time and resources to serve her Lord.

Mary Magdalene became Jesus' faithful follower, ministering with Him and the disciples and providing financial support. What a blessing to minister with Jesus Christ Himself! From deep personal gratitude she gave all of her time and resources to serve her Lord.

When Mary Magdalene saw Jesus after His resurrection, she called Him Rabboni (see John 20:16), the strongest expression of reverent love. _Rabboni_ means _teacher_ or _master_. Mary Magdalene was grateful for Christ's gifts of salvation and healing. But she also loved Him because He was her teacher. She could never fully express her deep gratitude to Him.

Think of persons who teach or minister to you. List their names and thank God for them.

_____

Have you thanked these persons lately? Call them or write notes.

GRATEFUL IN DEVOTION

Each of the four Gospels gives an account of Mary Magdalene's presence at the cross. Her devotion to Jesus kept her with Him even when other followers left (see Mark 15:40-41). Her loyalty and consistency were expressions of gratitude for all Jesus had done for her.

Read all four accounts of the resurrection and explain what they imply about Mary Magdalene's personal character and deep gratitude to Jesus Christ.

Matthew 28:1-10: _____

_____

Mark 16:1-11: _____

_____

Luke 24:1-12: _____

_____

John 20:1-18: _____

85

_____

Each account mentions Mary Magdalene's name first. In Matthew she publicly demonstrated her devotion to Christ despite possible consequences. Mark's Gospel describes Mary Magdalene's service and loyalty. Luke's brief account confirms Mary Magdalene's great faith and bold witness. John's Gospel focuses on Mary Magdalene as the first to discover the empty tomb and to tell about Christ's resurrection after He appeared to her. Each account attests to Mary Magdalene's deep love for and gratitude to Jesus.

Like Mary Magdalene, Christian women today should maintain a deep sense of gratitude toward God all the time. A spirit of gratitude is not a part of human nature. It is a behavior that must be learned. Just as children must be taught to say thank you, Christians must be taught to be grateful. Here are some ways you can learn to be grateful to God:

- Gratitude begins with a focus on God, not self. Recognize that God is the source of everything good (see Jas. 1:17).
- Be grateful even for small things. Look for blessings to be thankful for; sometimes blessings are not obvious.
- Express your thanksgiving to God privately and publicly. Public prayers can be a witness to others (see John 11:41-42).
- Be grateful to God even in the midst of suffering.

Do you have an attitude of gratitude? One way to express your thankfulness to God is to keep a gratitude journal. Each day write five things you are grateful for. Begin now by writing in the margin five things you are grateful for today.

Mary Magdalene truly had an attitude of gratitude for God's mercy toward her. She expressed her gratitude in many ways. She gave everything she had to Christ and faithfully followed Him. She remained with Him through His death and resurrection. Let Mary Magdalene's attitude of gratitude inspire you to remain ever grateful for all God is and for all He does for you.

Christian women today should maintain a deep sense of gratitude toward God all the time.

DAY 4
THE HEMORRHAGING WOMAN
A STRONG BELIEVER

THIS WEEK'S LIFE VERSE
"As the sufferings of Christ abound in us, so our consolation also abounds through Christ" (2 Cor. 1:5).

TODAY'S LIFE LESSON
Strength

TODAY'S BACKGROUND SCRIPTURES
Matthew 9:20-22
Mark 5:25-34
Luke 8:43-48

Have you ever been desperate or without hope? Sometimes chronic pain or illness can make you feel hopeless. Three of the Gospels relate the story of a woman who was desperate because she had been bleeding continuously for 12 years. The Bible does not name her, but it consistently describes her as a woman with a flow of blood. Let's call her the hemorrhaging woman.

Read today's background Scriptures, Matthew 9:20-22; Mark 5:25-34; Luke 8:43-48.

A PERSISTENT ILLNESS
The exact cause of this woman's bleeding is uncertain, but the duration is clearly stated. A chronic, lingering illness takes a great toll on a person and can lead to isolation and depression. The hemorrhaging woman must have been weak and in pain. Even today, with the advances in medical science, chronic illness is debilitating.

Name a chronic physical, emotional, or spiritual problem you have. How does that persistent problem affect you?

_____

Scripture says that the hemorrhaging woman went to doctor after doctor but found no relief. As a result, she suffered financially as well as physically. She suffered socially and mentally because her unclean status made her a social outcast. Spiritually, however, she was strong. While obviously discouraged, she had great faith in God. The strong faith of this weak woman brought healing by Jesus Christ. Jesus provides cleansing for the unclean.

Many believers today have debilitating illnesses. But as Christians, they can lean on the Lord for strength and can remain open to His work in their lives even when the doctors are unable to help.

A MIRACULOUS HEALING
Jesus healed several women during His earthly ministry. The hemorrhaging woman was different from the others because she was considered unclean. According to Old Testament law, the hemorrhaging woman could not enter God's presence or be touched by a Jew. Physical contact would make the other person unclean.

This strong Jewish tradition adds to the significance of the woman's healing. The hemorrhaging woman was desperate. She knew the risks of her presence in public, but she was determined to see Jesus anyway. She knew that He was at risk if He touched her, but she was confident that only Jesus Christ could heal her. So she braved the crowds and touched His garment. Jesus, aware of her tender touch, healed the hemorrhaging woman at that moment. She was healed immediately.

Read Luke 8:48. What did Jesus say to the woman after He had healed her?

87

_____

_____

What is Jesus saying to you now about your chronic problem?

_____

_____

God does not always heal physical problems, but He always strengthens and works His will in those who reach out to Him in faith. He encourages believers to pray for healing and to pray for others who are sick. In spite of the circumstances, Christians can rejoice because God is in control and wants to work His will in them. First Thessalonians 5:18 strengthens the faith of a wounded believer. Read that verse in the margin.

"Be cheerful no matter what; pray all the time; thank God no matter what happens. This is the way God wants you who belong to Christ to live" (1 Thess. 5:18, The Message).

A Strong Faith

When the hemorrhaging woman touched the hem of Jesus' garment, He asked aloud, "Who touched Me?" Don't you know that this weak woman was frightened? If she answered aloud, the crowd would recognize her as unclean. If she did not confess her action, Jesus would know anyway. So she humbly knelt before Him and sought His mercy. Her faith pleased Jesus. He publicly affirmed her faith.

In Matthew 9:22 and Luke 8:48 Jesus called the woman daughter. What does that term of endearment say about their relationship? Jesus acknowledged the hemorrhaging woman as His child. Any person who trusts God in faith for salvation is a child of God, His precious loved one.

The Luke account records that the woman "declared to Him in the presence of all the people the reason she had touched Him and how she was healed immediately" (Luke 8:47). The woman testified to others about what Jesus had done for her! Women today can do the same about God's work in their lives. As God strengthens you in your pain, you should seek to strengthen others. As you reach out to others when you are hurting, God brings healing to your heart even when physical healing is not within His will. When wounded women today are blessed with physical, emotional, and spiritual healing, they have the joy of sharing that testimony with others.

What healing has God brought in your life about which you can testify to others?

_____

_____

_____

88

DAY 5
THE WOMAN AT THE WELL
FROM BONDAGE TO FREEDOM

THIS WEEK'S LIFE VERSE
"As the sufferings of Christ abound in us, so our consolation also abounds through Christ" (2 Cor. 1:5).

TODAY'S LIFE LESSON
Freedom

TODAY'S BACKGROUND SCRIPTURE
John 4:5-30,39-42

Freedom, a common theme in Scripture, is contrasted with bondage in both the Old and New Testaments. Freedom is liberation from the control of another person or power,[11] and bondage is subjection to a force or an influence.[12] People in the Bible sought social, political, moral, and spiritual freedom. People today also desire freedom, though they often find themselves enslaved. As Christians we can have freedom in Christ. Because of Jesus Christ we are no longer slaves to sin (see John 8:34) but "slaves of God" (Rom. 6:22). This spiritual freedom is eternal!

The woman at the well was a slave to sin until she met Jesus. This first-century sinner gratefully received the freedom offered to all people today through faith in Jesus Christ.

Read today's background Scripture, John 4:5-30,39-42.

FREEDOM FROM SELF

Little is known personally about the nameless Samaritan woman who encountered Jesus at Jacob's well in Sychar, but much can be inferred about her from her background. Eight times she is referred to as "the woman," and one time Jesus calls her "Woman." His speaking to her is significant because in the patriarchal society of Jesus' day women were considered greatly inferior to men. A man did not speak to a woman in public, not even to his wife, mother, or sister. The woman's role was restricted primarily to the home and family.

Why do you think Jesus broke cultural rules and spoke to this woman?

_____

_____

Jesus Christ recognized the worth of women. Although He respected Hebrew tradition throughout His ministry, He elevated the status of women. Jesus offered salvation to women, He ministered with women, and He worked supernaturally in the lives of women. Through public recognition of her womanhood, Jesus offered the woman at the well personal freedom. In Christ, women today can experience freedom from the bondage of self. Their personal limitations and weaknesses can be forgiven, and their lives can become vessels for service. Freedom from self is one of the greatest freedoms Christ offers.

Have you thought about the obstacles self poses to a close relationship with God? Identify the ungodly desires and fleshly strengths that keep you from relying on and submitting to God.

_____

_____

Freedom from self is one of the greatest freedoms Christ offers.

89

FREEDOM FROM PREJUDICE

The fact that Jesus' encounter with this women took place in Samaria is shocking. Since Jews did not speak to Samaritans, they often avoided the area. Believing that the Samaritans, who had intermarried with foreigners, had betrayed their faith, Jews regarded the Samaritans with hatred and prejudice. Jesus reached across racial barriers, offering the woman forgiveness and freedom. He also ministered to other Samaritans and taught His disciples to love them. Christians today can learn from Jesus how to overcome racial boundaries.

Read the following Scriptures. Then draw lines across the columns to match the references with Jesus' teachings about the Samaritans.

Luke 9:51-56	Many Samaritans believed that Jesus is the Savior.
Luke 10:30-37	Jesus told a parable about a good Samaritan.
Luke 17:11-16	Jesus told the disciples to spread the good news to Samaria.
John 4:39-42	Jesus rebuked the disciples when they wanted to destroy the Samaritans.
Acts 1:8	A Samaritan leper thanked Jesus for healing him.

90

Prayer Guide
- Pray for freedom from the bondage of self, paying particular attention to your list on page 89.
- Examine your heart in regard to racial prejudice. Confess any sin and let Christ's love govern your thoughts and actions in the future.
- If you are a victim of prejudice, ask for God's strength and an abiding sense of His love for you.
- Confess sins that hold you in bondage.
- Meditate on these verses: " 'You shall know the truth, and the truth shall make you free' " (John 8:32). " 'I am the way, the truth, and the life' " (John 14:6). Now thank God for freedom from sin and for the Truth, Jesus Christ.

Christ's love transcends racial boundaries. By offering the Samaritan woman His love, Jesus freed her from the bondage of racial prejudice. The same freedom is available to women today.

FREEDOM FROM SIN

The Samaritan woman was immoral. Living in an adulterous relationship, she was a social outcast. She was trapped in a lifestyle taking her farther from God and isolating her from people. Unlike the other women, she went to the well at noon to avoid their judgmental stares.

Though Jesus knew this sinful woman's history, He chose to reveal Himself to her anyway so that He could set her free spiritually. His approach is a model of effective witnessing. He responded to her in a way she could understand. Knowing that she had come to the well for water to quench her physical thirst, Jesus gave her living water to quench her spiritual thirst. The woman recognized His divinity, calling Him a prophet; gratefully accepted His living water; and received everlasting life. She went to the well as a slave to sin and walked away a free woman in Christ!

Review John 4:39-42. What did the woman do after believing in Christ?

_____

The excited woman told the Samaritans in town about her encounter with Jesus. Because of her testimony, many became believers.

The woman at the well experienced the freedom that only Christ can give. Today He offers wounded women the same freedom from self, prejudice, and sin. That is true hope in a hurting world.

To end this study, spend time in prayer, following the prayer guide in the margin.

---

[1]Dorothy Kelley Patterson and Rhonda Harrington Kelley, eds., *The Woman's Study Bible* (Nashville: Thomas Nelson Publishers, 1995), 33.

[2]David B. Guralnik, ed., *Webster's New World Dictionary of the American Language,* 2nd college ed. (New York: The World Publishing Company, 1970), 1288.

[3]Patterson and Kelley, *The Woman's Study Bible,* 33.

[4]James Orr, ed., *The International Standard Bible Encyclopedia* (Grand Rapids: Wm. B. Eerdmans Publishing Co., 1960), 1316.

[5]Herbert Lockyer, *All the Women of the Bible* (Grand Rapids: Zondervan Publishing House, n.d.), 64.

[6]Adapted from Edith Deen, *All of the Women of the Bible* (San Francisco: HarperCollins Publishers, 1955), 264-66.

[7]Adapted from Trent Butler, ed., *Holman Bible Dictionary* (Nashville: Holman Bible Publishers, 1991), 1170-71.

[8]Guralnik, *Webster's New World Dictionary of the American Language,* 610.

[9]Butler, *Holman Bible Dictionary,* 1336.

[10]Lockyer, *All the Women of the Bible,* 100.

[11]Guralnik, *Webster's New World Dictionary of the American Language,* 556.

[12]Ibid., 160.

LEADER GUIDE

This leader guide will help you facilitate six group sessions. Each weekly session is designed to be one hour in length. Feel free to follow the suggestions in this guide, but do not let them restrict you. Be responsive to the Holy Spirit and sensitive to the needs of the women in your group.

Distribute books at least one week in advance or conduct a brief introductory session to overview the study and to distribute books. Group session 1 should follow members' completion of week 1 in this book.

SESSION 1

WOMEN IN THE BIBLE

REVIEW TIME (5 mins.)

Introduce yourself and have members do the same. Read this week's life verse, Acts 9:36. Ask volunteers to share "good works and charitable deeds" they have done. Give God the glory!

SHARING TIME (50 mins.)

1. Have women name Bible women they relate to and state why.
2. Ask if any women were named after Bible women and what those names mean.
3. Discuss the meaning of *faith* and summarize Ruth's life of faith.
4. Emphasize that faith is chosen, not inherited. Ask women to name ways they share their faith and ways their faith influences their actions.
5. Ask women to compare wisdom and knowledge. List responses on the chalkboard. State that wisdom is a gift from God. Recall Abigail's wisdom in dealing with David.
6. Ask women to share times when God gave them wisdom to offer help or deal with difficult situations.
7. Invite members to describe times when they

rebelled against God as Gomer did. Explain that hope lies in repenting and turning to God. Hold a time of silent prayer for repentance, broken relationships, and persons who need to find hope in God's redemption.
8. Lead the group in a discussion of spiritual gifts. Have women name their spiritual gifts. Write these on the chalkboard.
9. State that God wants us to use our spiritual gifts for His glory as Mary and Martha used theirs. Have women identify specific ways they can use the gifts listed on the chalkboard.
10. Read aloud the account of Dorcas in Acts 9: 36-42. Ask women to discuss ways to show generosity to others.
11. Focus on God's generosity to us. Have women identify His blessings to them.

PRAYER TIME (5 mins.)

1. Ask women which Christian virtue they need to develop most—faith, wisdom, hope, worship, service, or generosity. Divide into small groups based on those prayer needs and spend time in prayer together. Close by praying that women will hear and understand what God says to them through this study and that they will be committed to obeying Him.
2. Encourage each woman to choose a prayer partner from the group. Ask partners to contact each other during the week to share concerns and praises and to support each other in their daily study.

SESSION 2

WIVES IN THE BIBLE

REVIEW TIME (5 mins.)

Read aloud together this week's life verse, Luke 1:42. Ask members to explain what it means to be "blessed among women." Then have them turn to each other and say, You are blessed!

Sharing Time (50 mins.)

1. Encourage any single women to participate in this group session regardless of their marital status. Point out that these biblical examples can teach them how to practice godly virtues in other relationships and how to submit to God, love Him, and be faithful to Him. Be sensitive to single women as you lead the discussion.

2. Lead a brief discussion of the biblical role of wives. Conclude by quoting Proverbs 18:22: "He who finds a wife finds a good thing."

3. Discuss Sarah's submission to God and Abraham. Ask women to describe the consequences when Sarah took matters into her own hands. Ask: Have you ever tried to manipulate God's plan? What happened?

4. Ask volunteers to share their struggles with submission to their husbands and to God.

5. Discuss the kindness of Rebekah and the consequences when her kindness got out of balance.

6. Ask women to name kind gestures that are meaningful to them. Encourage them to be more intentional in showing kindness to their husbands and to others.

7. Review the life of Rachel. Have women describe covenant relationships, specifically the love of a wife for her husband.

8. Ask women to discuss how love can sustain a couple through sorrow. State that God's love never fails, even in difficult times.

9. Ask women to name ways Elizabeth affirmed others. Ask, What words of affirmation have you spoken lately? Encourage women to plan one encouraging comment to make to their husbands or someone significant in their lives. Challenge women to consider being spiritual mentors to other women.

10. Ask women to recall the time spent with their husbands this week and to discuss what they can do to spend more time together. Ask single women to apply this idea to significant persons in their lives with whom they spend time.

11. Remind women that companionship with God as a couple is important. Ask for testimonies about couple quiet times. Challenge women to discuss with their husbands the importance of couple time in Bible study and prayer.

12. Have married women write love notes to their husbands. Ask single women to write notes of appreciation to couples they know who set godly examples of marriage.

Prayer Time (5 mins.)

Pray specifically for marriages. Ask women to write down names of couples who need prayer for God to restore their marriages. Spend time in individual prayer for group members' marriages and for the marriages of others.

Session 3

Mothers in the Bible

Review Time (5 mins.)

Have women silently read this week's life verses, 1 Samuel 1:27-28. Ask members, Have you given your children to the Lord? Ask them to share ways God is already using their children for His glory.

Sharing Time (50 mins.)

1. Remind any childless women that they can use these lessons to influence the children with whom they have opportunities to interact. Be sensitive to childless women as you lead the discussion.

2. Read aloud Genesis 2:18-25. Ask, How are women God's special creation?

3. Invite women to react to these statements from week 3, day 1: "Although Eve was 'the mother of all living,' she was also the mother of all dying. Through her life and lineage both sin and grace entered the world." Conclude the discussion by saying, "While Eve's life teaches the wages of sin, Eve also exemplifies God's grace to forgive and restore His children."

4. Discuss blessings and challenges of motherhood. Pray for children who have rebelled against God.

5. Discuss ways Hannah was devoted to her husband, to God, and to her son. Emphasize the importance of dedicating children to the Lord.

6. Ask volunteers to share their earliest childhood memories of their mothers. Thank God for devoted mothers like Hannah.

7. Ask women to recall ways their mothers-in-law and other women have influenced their lives as Naomi influenced Ruth. Ask, What can you do to show love to your mother-in-law?

8. Review on page 42 the list of requirements for friendship. Ask, Is there anything you would add? Challenge women to use these suggestions to build friendships through which they can influence other women.

9. Review the ways Mary taught Jesus to be obedient to God's call, to thirst for knowledge, and to love people. Ask volunteers to share ways they answered the questions on pages 44–45 about teaching their children in these ways.

10. Ask women to identify ways Lois and Eunice nurtured Timothy in his faith. Have women identify ways they can nurture their children or grandchildren spiritually. List these on the chalkboard as they are discussed.

11. Ask volunteers to share their paraphrases of Proverbs 22:6 (see p. 48).

Prayer Time (5 mins.)

1. Give a three-by-five-inch card to each woman and ask her to write the names of children, grandchildren, or special children in her life. She should also write one prayer request for each child. Ask women to exchange cards and to pray silently for the children's needs listed.

2. Close by encouraging women to continue the supportive relationships they have built with their prayer partners.

Session 4
Working Women in the Bible

Review Time (5 mins.)

Ask someone to read aloud this week's life verse, 1 Corinthians 15:58. Discuss how Christian women can be steadfast and immovable in the workplace.

Sharing Time (50 mins.)

1. Ask women to brainstorm the greatest challenges facing working women. List these on the chalkboard.

2. Discuss the meaning of *integrity*. Ask women what made Huldah a prophetess of integrity.

3. Ask: What does it mean to live a life of integrity? How can working women have integrity today?

4. Have women identify and discuss the primary characteristics of the Proverbs 31 woman (diligent, determined, disciplined). Write them on the chalkboard. Ask women to suggest ways these characteristics can help them meet the challenges working women face, listed earlier.

5. Discuss the meaning of divine discipline. Call on volunteers to read their ideas of ways to develop it (see p. 55).

6. Ask a volunteer to explain the differences between happiness and joy. Ask women to describe times when they had cause to rejoice like Rhoda, such as when prayers were answered.

7. Ask: What keeps you from experiencing joy on the job? What can you do to experience the joy of the Lord in your daily routine?

8. Ask: What were Lydia's priorities after she was saved? How did her actions reflect her priorities? What can working women do to ensure that they maintain the proper priorities?

9. Ask prayer partners to examine together their rankings of priorities on page 60. Ask them to discuss their struggles with priorities and to pray together about placing God first.

10. Ask women to name skills Priscilla possessed. List these on the chalkboard and ask, How did Priscilla use her skills in ministry? Now ask women to share skills they have. Discuss how they can use those skills as Priscilla did to serve the Lord.

PRAYER TIME (5 mins.)

Ask women to rewrite 1 Corinthians 15:58 as individual prayers of commitment. Then ask them to pray those prayers silently.

SESSION 5

WOMEN LEADERS IN THE BIBLE

REVIEW TIME (5 mins.)

Have several members read this week's life verse, Esther 4:14, from different Bible translations. Ask for testimonies of occasions when group members have performed significant ministry tasks at strategic times.

SHARING TIME (50 mins.)

1. Ask women to name characteristics that made Miriam an effective leader. List these on the chalkboard. Ask, Are these qualities still important for women in leadership today? Point out the list of leadership characteristics on page 65 that women can use for self-assessment.

2. Ask: What happened when Miriam no longer followed God's direction? What evidence do we have that Miriam's leadership role was later restored? Emphasize the importance of leaders' reliance on God and of letting Him lead through them.

3. Ask women to name Deborah's many accomplishments as a judge. List these in a column on the chalkboard beside the list you made for Miriam. Ask, What made Deborah so effective as a leader? (Her pronouncements were just and authoritative because they were from God.)

4. State, One way God dispenses justice is through believers who hold positions of leadership. Ask, Are you dealing justly with others through your leadership role?

5. Have women list characteristics of Esther. Write these beside the other lists on the chalkboard. Point out that Esther's courage was fueled by her compassion and concern for her people.

6. Ask women to identify ways they can express compassion and courage in their leadership roles.

7. Read the account of Anna in Luke 2:36-38. Ask women to name qualities of her leadership. Add these to the qualities listed on the chalkboard.

8. Point out that Anna's dignity resulted from her godliness and her association with God's work. She hungered for the things of God and for the coming of the Messiah. Ask, How can women in leadership today serve with dignity as Anna did?

9. Review the leadership roles played by women in the early church (see the opening paragraphs in day 5). State that like them, we have a model for humble service in Jesus Christ.

10. Have women name the leadership characteristics of Phoebe and Damaris. List these on the chalkboard beside the other lists. Emphasize that humble service originates in the confession that we can do nothing without God. As we lead, we must remain totally dependent on Him and must follow His direction.

PRAYER TIME (5 mins.)

Give women time to examine the five lists of leadership characteristics on the chalkboard. Ask prayer partners to share with each other the qualities they most need to develop as leaders and to pray together about what God wants them to be as leaders.

SESSION 6
WOUNDED WOMEN IN THE BIBLE

REVIEW TIME (5 mins.)
Briefly discuss the suffering Christian women may experience today. Ask, Why do Christians suffer? Have volunteers read James 1:2-4 and 1 Peter 1:6-7. Read aloud this week's life verse, 2 Corinthians 1:5, and ask a volunteer to restate it in her own words.

SHARING TIME (50 mins.)
1. Discuss God's provision for Hagar. Ask: What causes insecurity for women today? How does God provide security for wounded women today?
2. Briefly review the tragedies of Dinah and Tamar. Ask: How does it feel to be an innocent victim? What help does God provide for those who have been hurt?
3. Ask, What is the Christian response to those who wrong us? Make sure the biblical teachings on page 83 are mentioned.
4. Discuss the ways Mary Magdalene demonstrated her gratitude to Jesus. List these on the chalkboard.
5. Review ways we can learn to be grateful to God (p. 85). Ask women to identify what they are grateful for today.
6. Ask, What made the difference in bringing healing to the hemorrhaging woman? (faith) State that today many people are healed when they reach out to God in faith.
7. State, God does not always choose to bring healing, but if we continually yield our hearts to Him, He gives us strength and works His will in us to make us what He wants us to be. Ask, What blessings can result from our suffering? List responses on the chalkboard.
8. Allow prayer partners to share their needs for healing and to pray about these needs. If time permits, they may also wish to identify and pray for other wounded women.

9. Discuss the dimensions of freedom the woman at the well experienced.
10. Ask women to discuss what freedom in Christ means to them.

PRAYER TIME (5 mins.)
Consider some of the following suggestions for reflection and commitment to end this study.
1. Allow members to share ways God has worked in their lives during the past six weeks.
2. Ask, What do you sense that God wants you to do next to continue growing?
3. Ask, What can we do to support one another? Consider meeting regularly as a group for encouragement and prayer or participating in another group study. Possibilities include:
   • *A Woman's Heart: God's Dwelling Place*
   • *A Heart like His: Seeking the Heart of God Through a Study of David*
   • *To Live Is Christ: The Life and Ministry of Paul*
   • *Living Beyond Yourself: Exploring the Fruit of the Spirit*
   • *Breaking Free: Making Liberty in Christ a Reality in Life*
   • *In My Father's House: Women Relating to God as Father*
   • *Whispers of Hope*
   For information about these products, contact Women's Enrichment Ministry Specialist, MSN 151; LifeWay Christian Resources; 127 Ninth Avenue, North; Nashville, TN 37234-0151. To order resources, write to Customer Service Center, MSN 113; 127 Ninth Avenue, North; Nashville, TN 37234-0113; fax (615) 251-5933; call toll free (800) 458-2772; email *customerservice@lifeway.com*; order online at *www.lifeway.com*; or visit a Lifeway Christian Store.
4. Have any ministry needs arisen that we want to organize to address?

   Close with prayer, dedicating your lives as women to Jesus and His service.

CHRISTIAN GROWTH STUDY PLAN

Preparing Christians to Serve

In the **Christian Growth Study Plan (formerly the Church Study Course),** this book, *Life Lessons from Women in the Bible,* is a resource for course credit in the subject area Personal Life in the Christian Growth category of diploma plans. To receive credit, read the book; complete the learning activities; attend group sessions; show your work to your pastor, a staff member, or a church leader; then complete the following information. This page may be duplicated. Send the completed page to:

Christian Growth Study Plan, MSN 117
127 Ninth Avenue, North
Nashville, TN 37234-0117
Fax: (615) 251-5067

For information about the Christian Growth Study Plan, refer to the current *Christian Growth Study Plan Catalog.* Your church office may have a copy. If not, request a free copy from the Christian Growth Study Plan office, (615) 251-2525.

Life Lessons from Women in the Bible
CG-0440

PARTICIPANT INFORMATION

Social Security Number (USA ONLY)	Personal CGSP Number*	Date of Birth (MONTH, DAY, YEAR)
– –	–	– –

Name (First, Middle, Last)		Home Phone
☐ Mr. ☐ Miss		
☐ Mrs. ☐		– –

Address (Street, Route, or P.O. Box)	City, State, or Province	Zip/Postal Code

CHURCH INFORMATION

Church Name

Address (Street, Route, or P.O. Box)	City, State, or Province	Zip/Postal Code

CHANGE REQUEST ONLY

☐ Former Name

☐ Former Address	City, State, or Province	Zip/Postal Code

☐ Former Church	City, State, or Province	Zip/Postal Code

Signature of Pastor, Conference Leader, or Other Church Leader	Date

*New participants are requested but not required to give SS# and date of birth. Existing participants, please give CGSP# when using SS# for the first time.
Thereafter, only one ID# is required. **Mail to:** Christian Growth Study Plan, 127 Ninth Ave., North, Nashville, TN 37234-0117. Fax: (615)251-5067